Simply Quince

Pinnacle
Book Achievement
Award

Barbara Ghazarian

Simply Quince

barbara ghazarian

Mayreni Publishing

Mayreni Publishing's books may be purchased for educational, business, or sales
promotional use. For more information, please contact Mayreni Publishing.

First Edition

Food Stylist: Kimberly Kissling
Assistant Food Stylist: Sarah Fairhurst
Food Photography: Dan Mills
Illustrations: Craig Wallen
Cover Design: Christopher Fucile
Book Design: Vatche Ghazarian

Printed on acid-free paper in Canada

Library of Congress Control Number: 2008946746

Ghazarian, Barbara
   Simply Quince/Barbara Ghazarian

      p. cm.
         ISBN-13: 978-1-931834-31-5
         ISBN-10: 1-931834-31-8
         1.   Cookery (Quince)   2. Quince

DEDICATION

To the Armenian people, who, like quince, are rooted in the same homeland soil and have endured through the ages; and to John Kaprielian and the Kaprielian family of Fresno County, California. The Kaprielians planted quince on their family farm in 1919 and have faithfully cultivated the ancestral fruit through good times and bad.

Also by Barbara Ghazarian
Simply Armenian: Naturally Healthy Ethnic Cooking Made Easy
Descendants of Noah: Christian Stories from the Armenian Heart

CONTENTS

Acknowledgments

No one writes a cookbook alone. It boggles my mind when I think of the number of people who have helped and supported me with this project. Quince lovers who emerged from all walks of life and diverse interests—family, friends and neighbors, professional chefs, foodies, orchardists, and gardeners—all enthusiastically embraced Team Quince and began working to secure the near-forgotten heirloom quince a place in the garden and on the contemporary table. I am grateful for the support and encouragement they shared with me from conception to completion of this project.

Thank you to John Kaprielian of Kaprielian Brothers in Reedley, California. John generously provided bushels and bushels of commercial-grade fresh quince from three harvests. Without fresh fruit, I could not have developed, tested, and retested the recipes in this collection. His embracing me as a friend and adopted family member is an added bonus.

I must also identify a few people whose guidance, handholding, and wisdom were available in the trenches. I called these folks too many times to count, and every time they dropped what they were doing to help me. To them, I am humbly appreciative.

Craig Wallen, cousin extraordinaire, who deserves more credit than this mention, was my main recipe consultant. An avid foodie, Craig answered the phone every time I called, offered ingredient suggestions, shared recipes, tested recipes, tasted recipes, reviewed the manuscript, and applied an artistic eye during the design of this book. Thank you, Craig. I could not have accomplished this without your help.

John Karbowski, executive chef of Pampas Restaurant in Palo Alto, California, for his invaluable recipe consultations throughout the development process.

Carolyn Hill, longtime manager of the Burbank Farmers' Market and oracle of wisdom on all food topics from planting to harvest to the table.

Elaine Kesler, volunteer prep chef, farmer's daughter, and human peeling-and-slicing machine even with infant Benjamin propped in a bouncy chair nearby.

For help preparing the manuscript, I give heartfelt thanks to my readers Carolyn Hill, Chef John Karbowski, Rhonda Redden, and Craig Wallen. Also to Carolyn North Haley—a more talented mechanical editor I have yet to meet.

I am grateful to Dan Mills for his generous donation to The Culinary Trust of the International Association of Culinary Professionals, without which it would have been out of financial reach to secure the mouthwatering visuals in this book. Dan suggested the amazing food stylist Kim Kissling, who loved the idea from the beginning and led our team with insight.

Special thanks to my friends Lisa and Chris Fucile, who openheartedly offered their stunning kitchen and amazing photographic and design talents.

Many thanks also to Joseph Postman and Lon J. Rombough for their guidance on quince horticulture.

I thank my friends and neighbors in Pacific Grove, California, and Middletown, Rhode Island, who were always willing to taste my recipe attempts and give honest feedback. Your responses helped enormously and made cooking much more fun.

Finally, I thank my husband and daughter, who both ate quince for many moons without complaint.

INTRODUCTION

I am passionate about quince.

"What?" most folks ask." You're passionate about what?"

Quince.

"Spell it?"

Q-U-I-N-C-E.

"Fifteen? You're passionate about the number fifteen?" said a Spanish-speaking friend, puzzled, thinking me a gringa trying to communicate.

"Not *quince* (keen-say). *Membrillo* (mem-bree-oh)," I said in my most articulate Spanish.

"Ah! Membrillo. I love membrillo."

Marmelo in Portuguese, *coing* in French, *quitte* in German, *ayva* in Turkish, and *sergevil* in Armenian—across the globe, the fruit-bearing quince tree (*Cydonia oblonga*) is cultivated and prized for its versatility in the kitchen. But here in the United States, the quince has been nearly forgotten.

It's hard to imagine a time when this fragrant relative of the apple and pear was a centerpiece on the American table. But the astringent fruit was so valued for its high pectin content and aromatic flavor that Puritan settlers brought it to New England in 1629. Quince trees flourished in yards and gardens throughout the colonies, and colonial cooks prepared quince jams, jellies, compotes, and pies for their families in the fall. Within a century, however, the apple snatched the spotlight and the popularity of quince steadily declined. The development of artificial pectin in the midtwentieth century sealed the quince's fate. Today the fruit is considered a rare, specialty fruit.

Why, then, after generations of obscurity, should I profess a passion for the quince?

Sometimes I romanticize that this passion runs through my veins along with my Armenian blood. The fruit first took root in historic Armenian soil, and today wild quince trees grow in the Caucasus Mountains of Armenia, Georgia, and northern Iran.

More likely, my infatuation was kindled when I was a child. Everyone in my family was weaned on Grandma's delicious ruby-red quince preserves. Quince trees grew in the yard, and every fall during the final days of September, my grandmother watched the fruit for signs of ripening. She taught me that the rock-hard fruit was ready for picking when its fuzzy green skin turned yellow and its heady, roselike fragrance permeated the neighborhood. Then my five-foot-tall-in-heels grandmother headed out into the yard with a step stool to pick the sun-ripened fruit from the tangled branches.

For days before she made her preserves and jelly, baskets brimming with ripening quince would sit in the hallway and the aroma of quince filled the house. In ancient times, Greeks placed ripe quinces in their rooms as fresheners.

After my grandmother passed away, I gladly took on the family tradition of *quincing*—with one major difference: I invited other cooks to participate.

Autumn quincing events a became tradition in my home, and each year I expanded my repertoire to include unique salads, savory stews, scrumptious sides, condiments for roasted meats, and a wide variety of desserts—lots and lots of desserts—all perfect for holiday feasts and gift giving.

Exploring the versatility of the quince in the kitchen required jumping hurdles. Only recently have national food magazines published short articles on the quince, along with a handful of recipes. Unfortunately, many food writers begin by pitying the poor quince. They highlight the fruit's limited snacking appeal and hard, irregular, fuzz-blanketed shape. Invariably, they say that quince is notoriously hard to cut and core.

But if you're a home cook willing to make an apple pie, you're a cook who can add quince to your repertoire.

I wrote this book so that your exploration of this mysterious, ancient fruit will be easier than mine, and your results more assured. My recipes are simple, easy to prepare, and reliably delicious. They showcase the fruit's mild flavor, delicate aroma, and exotic look without making it fancy. Some dishes are sweet, others savory; all are scrumptious. All were tested, tweaked, retested, and served to tasters, and the process was repeated to perfection.

I recognize that many of you will be trying quince for the first time, so I want you to be successful on the first try. It's important to be organized and pace yourself when preparing quince, because it is the quintessential slow food.

Quince's astringent, pectin-rich raw pulp often requires cooking for more than 1 hour, to tenderize the fruit and bring out its subtle flavor and rich color. Numerous recipes call for Poached Quince as an ingredient (page 27), which requires preparation of the final dish to be done in stages over a two-day period. Your quincing archenemies are running out of time and mild fatigue. So plan ahead. Familiarize yourself with the entire recipe before beginning. Where applicable in a recipe, I have suggested breaks.

Organizing your kitchen and having the correct tools on hand are more important than usual when working with quince. Please read "ABOUT QUINCE AND COOKING WITH QUINCE" (page 18) and refer to KITCHEN TOOLS in the back of the book before starting my easy-to-follow, step-by-step instructions.

One of the best aspects of working with quince is that you can use the entire fruit—skin, core, flesh, and seeds. Whether you are a seasoned chef or home cook or you are new to quince, once you begin eating this fruit you may become obsessed with its versatility and flavor. If so, please join me and the increasing number of Team Quince members (page 195) in our efforts to reestablish the quince in the garden and on the table in the United States and around the world.

Simply Quince is a landmark in culinary history. It is the first cookbook ever published devoted exclusively to the quince. Armed with the unpretentious recipes found in this collection, together we can make more culinary history and champion the quintessential underdog of fruits.

Now, when someone asks, "What's a quince?" *Simply Quince* is the answer.

THE MIGRATION OF QUINCE THROUGH HISTORY

Some biblical scholars speculate that quince may have been the true forbidden fruit, tempting Eve with its golden tone and alluring aroma to try a bite. The "apple" in the Song of Solomon may have been a quince as well, along with the "apple" of most Western civilization myths. Homer, Virgil, Plutarch, Dioscordes, and other classical writers extolled the quince's virtues.

For millennia, quince played a central role in human history. Native to the Caucasus region, the fruit was first cultivated in Mesopotamia, an area now known as northern Iraq, between the Tigris and Euphrates rivers.

Between 200 and 100 BCE, this "golden apple" had spread to the eastern Mediterranean and Palestine.

The popularity and territorial boundaries of quince continued their eastward spread after 763 CE, when the Arabs moved their capital from Damascus (Syria) to the walled city of Baghdad. Ancient Baghdad bustled with multicultural activity, and trade expanded to Persia, India, and China. Traders brought rhubarb from China; coconuts from India; and quinces, apples, saffron, and salt from Persia. Quince remains a popular ingredient in Middle Eastern meat stews, especially with lamb, where it adds sweetness, astringency, and texture.

Quince Moves West

Mention of quince appears in Greek writings around 600 BCE. It became associated with both love and fertility. Lovers exchanged quinces as engagement tokens. Wedding cakes were flavored with quince, sesame, and honey, and quinces were tossed into the bridal chariot as symbols of fertility.

In Greek legend, Hercules was ordered to steal the Golden Apples (probably quinces) of the Hesperides for his eleventh labor; Eris, the goddess of strife, began the ill-fated beauty contest that resulted in Aphrodite giving Helen a quince that caused her to fall in love with Paris, thereby launching the Trojan War. Henceforth, the quince became known as the "Golden Apple of Discord" and identified with Aphrodite, the goddess of love.

There is a twelfth-century Greek recipe for quince honey. Translated into modern English, it instructs cooks to peel, core, and cut the fruit, then boil it in honey, adding pepper or ginger.

The quince traveled to Rome from Cydonia on the island of Crete. The Romans called it the Cydonia apple, which is how it picked up its botanical name, *Cydonia oblonga*. Pliny, the Roman naturalist and writer of the first century CE, mentioned the Mulvian variety, saying it could be eaten raw. Columella, another ancient naturalist, described three other varieties named the sparrow apple, the golden apple, and the must apple. The Romans also valued the quince for superstitious and medicinal purposes, such as averting the evil eye and aiding digestion. Quince blossoms were made into perfume, and the fruit was used to form the base of a hair dye.

Apicius, Rome's first cookbook author, preserved whole quinces with their stems and leaves attached in a bath of honey diluted with *defrutum*, a newly prepared spiced wine, in the first century CE. Other Roman recipes for quince included a kind of reduced wine, fish sauces, sauces for minced meat, and quince purée. Pompeiian frescoes depict quinces grasped in the paws of a bear.

Quince Enters Europe

Conquering Romans carried quince as far as the British Isles. Chaucer wrote of quince, using the name *coines*, a word derived from the French. In Middle English, *coine* was sometimes spelled *quyn*; the plural was *quyns*, the likely origin of our current name for the fruit.

Charlemagne seems to have come across quince during his campaign to spread Catholicism and conquer Western Europe, because in 812 he ordered a quince tree to be planted in the royal garden. And in 1429, when Joan of Arc broke the siege of

Orleans, the grateful citizens presented her with quince preserves, called *cotignac*, a local delicacy.

Throughout Medieval Europe, cooks spiced quince with pepper, ginger, cloves, cinnamon, and nutmeg. Quince dishes frequented menus at the Vatican. Food historians believe that the Arabs were probably the first to sweeten quinces with sugar, and that the Moors of North Africa introduced the custom to the Spanish and Portuguese. The best quinces available during that time came from Portugal. A variety named Portugal quince is grown in Europe today. The Portuguese word for quince is *marmelo*, and they made preserves called *marmalade*. Orange marmalade was first manufactured in Dundee, Scotland, in 1790, but until then, it was always made with quince.

In Tudor and Stuart times in England, quince marmalade, wrapped in gold foil, was regarded as an aphrodisiac. British cooks traditionally used quince to make tarts, preserves, and other sweets. In the eighteenth century, fledgling colonies in Australia and New Zealand depended on foods brought by ships from Britain. Although not documented, quince may have arrived by ship from England, but many food historians believe that the fruit may have traveled eastward from Persia, India, China, Japan, and finally south to the antipodes. Today, quince is cultivated and prized in both countries.

Quince Arrives in the New World

Quince crossed the Atlantic with Spanish and Portuguese sailors and settlers and was soon growing in the New World. Today the fruit grows in Mexico, Peru, Chile, Argentina, and Uruguay, where it is often eaten raw, sprinkled with salt and lime juice or hot salsa, and also cooked into sweet preserves and compotes.

Less than a decade after settling in New England, the Puritans requested quince seedlings from England. By 1720, quince was thriving throughout the colonies. It was commonly believed that pregnant women who indulged their appetites in generous quantities of quince would give birth to industrious, intelligent children. Gardening and cookbooks published during the next 200 years frequently mentioned the tree fruit as an easily obtainable staple. Through the nineteenth century, quince syrup was a popular soda-fountain drink.

Records from the 1850s report quince growing in Texas. Finally, the fruit made its way to California, where interest in breeding new varieties peaked in the late nineteenth century (see Cultivation and Varieties). But that was quince's last hurrah. Modern taste buds changed; the fruit was declared too hard and tart to eat raw, its pulp too difficult to cut, and cooking requirements too time consuming. I wrote this book to dispel these beliefs, as you will see from the recipes in this collection.

When I hold the solid weight of a fresh quince in my hand, close my eyes, and relax into its soft, floral fragrance, the amazing continuity of this ancient fruit becomes tangible. Maybe you, too, will be enticed to rediscover this old favorite, now that you know the role quince has played in human history.

About Quince and Cooking with Quince

Quince is often described by chefs and food writers as a cross between the apple and the pear. Although the analogy is valid with respect to appearance, ripening season, and genetics, it doesn't address the quince's unique qualities. For instance:

1. Quince is rarely, if ever, eaten raw. Do so and your mouth will pucker!

> There are folks who eat hand-picked quince. A woman I met at a farmers' market buying pineapple quince insisted that when bitten into like an apple, the fruit was sweet and juicy; only when cut with a knife did it become woody and astringent.
>
> The palatability of raw quince is the subject of copious, culinary legends.

2. Ripe quince is more aromatic than apple or pear; its fragrance is more like pineapple or guava.
3. Quince is the quintessential slow-food fruit. You can't really overcook it. Unlike apples, quince is hard to cook into mush; the fruit stubbornly retains its composition and shape even when shredded like a carrot or finely chopped in a

food processor. But with longer cooking times at low temperatures, the fruit darkens in color, from golden to salmon to pink to ruby red and finally to garnet. And the pectin-filled cell walls soften with increased cooking, so the fruit tenderizes. Undercooked quince is chewy, slightly astringent, and a bland yellow color.

Why does quince change color when cooked? For years I searched for an answer. Finally, I found it in Harold McGee's award-winning book *On Food and Cooking: The Science and Lore of the Kitchen*, 2004. Thank you, Harold!

Refer to McGee's tome if you are interested in the nitty-gritty science, but basically, at the molecular level, quince pulp contains a high concentration of large, colorless, water-soluble compounds called *phenolic compounds*. These are valuable antioxidants. When heated, the large phenolic compounds break down and react with oxygen to create smaller compounds called *anthocyanins*. Anthocyanins are responsible for most of the red, purple, and blue colors in plants, including berries, cabbage, radishes, and pomegranates. Cooking quince, especially with a little lemon juice and sugar, produces natural, red-pigmented anthocyanins. Voila! Lush holiday-colored fruit appears; natural magic, rare and wonderful.

4. Quince is extremely high in good-for-you antioxidants—those body-protecting, cancer-fighting molecules that many people consider the most important ingredient for maintaining long-term health. Nutritional analysis reveals that quinces have two to three times as much vitamin C as apples and pears, respectively, and four times as much iron as apples.

According to food scientist Harold McGee, "Some apples have the antioxidant activity equivalent to the vitamin C in 30 equal portions of orange!" Quinces have more antioxidant activity than any apple!

5. Quince is high in natural pectin, which is a water-soluble substance found in the peels, cores, seeds, and pulp of fruits and is used to thicken jams, jellies, and preserves. Pectin chains shake loose when heated in water, and the release of those chains at the molecular level softens the fruit.

> A 2008 study published by the United Kingdom's Institute of Food Research found that the form of pectin that acts as a jelling agent in jam and jelly may block the progression of cancer.

6. The flesh of quince is lower in juice than either apples or pears. In addition, the fruit's core is irregularly positioned at the fruit's center, and it is grainy, hard, and unsavory. All of the core must be removed before cooking, because it will never break down! If the core is not completely removed, your dish will have unpleasant, gritty pieces, like bone fragments.

In Season

Late August through December.

Where to Buy

Ethnic markets with produce departments that specialize in Middle Eastern and Latino foods stock quinces in season. They often sell imported quince preserves year round. Specialty grocers like Whole Foods Market and farmers' markets are also reliable suppliers. Produce sections of many major supermarkets, especially those in ethnic neighborhoods, stock fresh quinces in the fall. If your store does not carry them, ask the produce manager to order you some fruit. The produce number for quince is usually 4447 (although this is subject to change). If you can't find fresh quince locally, consult SOURCES, for mail-order alternatives.

Peeling and Cutting Quince

Fresh off the tree, a quince is covered in fuzz that needs to be removed before you can peel the fruit. Commercially, quince is gently rubbed with brushes to remove the fuzz; in the home kitchen, gently rub the fuzz off with your thumb or a moistened, thin kitchen towel. I often remove the down under running water, washing the fruit simultaneously.

Because the fruit is irregularly shaped, squaring it will make peeling and cutting easier. With a sharp knife, cut off the top and the bottom close to the stem. Don't worry about salvaging every bit of usable fruit. (But if thrift is in your nature, cover the discarded flesh, peels, and cores with lemon water and use them as a base for jelly.) You can also harvest and dry the seeds for medicinal purposes (page 35).

Unlike an apple, a quince is too bumpy, lumpy, and valleyed to peel in a circular motion. You'll get best results from using a broad-bladed potato peeler instead of a thin vegetable peeler. Starting from the stem-side top (generally smaller in diameter than the base), remove the peel by making confident downward strokes, working around the fruit's circumference. After peeling, check and remove all blemishes. Quinces bruise easily, which is why commercially grown quinces are picked and packed by hand.

You are now ready to quarter and core the fruit. Again unlike apples, quince cores tend to be irregularly shaped and off center, so an apple corer won't do the job. You will need to cut. Select a sturdy, sharp knife (I like a fruit knife), set the blemish-free, peeled fruit top-side up on a cutting surface, and quarter the fruit, with an eye to cutting around the core once you locate it. Note that it is easier to cut around the core than through it.

Once you have quartered the quince, completely remove its core with a sharp melon baller, paring knife, or peach pitter (see Kitchen Tools). A peach pitter is the most unusual tool in the quince kitchen, but the most useful.

Selection

Choose fruits that are more yellow than green and feel heavy for their size. Don't worry about bruises; they are only surface deep and can be trimmed. Size is not a factor in flavor, but large, smooth fruit is easier to cut than small or knobby specimens.

Varieties

More than two dozen varieties of quince have been documented, but only a few varieties are widely grown and commercially available (see CULTIVATION AND VARIETIES). Pineapple quince is the most popular. Quince of any variety can be used to prepare the recipes in this collection.

Size

Quinces vary greatly in size; I've provided a size chart (see page 23 and WEIGHTS AND MEASURES) that should help. All quantities of fresh quince needed in a recipe have been denoted by weight. Therefore, a food scale that can weigh up to 5 pounds is a critical quince kitchen tool. Numbers of fruit and cup measure are suggested when appropriate for clarity.

> Quince is quince no matter what size. All quinces taste and cook the same. The larger the fruit the greater amount of fruit pulp relative to core. In general, this ratio decreases with the size of the fruit. If your fruit tends to be smaller, you may need ¼ to ½ pounds more than what's called for in order to get the cups of fruit required for the dish.

Ripening and Storage

Quinces continue to ripen after harvesting and become increasingly golden yellow. If you are planning to use the fruit within a week or two, ripen it uncovered in a bowl. Quince makes an attractive, aromatic centerpiece when set on the table.

Otherwise, place quince in a cool (34°F to 58°F), dry place, out of direct sunlight, such as a cellar, garage, or pantry, and turn the fruit occasionally. I've kept fresh quince

Fresh Quince Size Chart

	Weight	Comparative Size	Pulp Equivalent (cups)
Large	9 oz. to >1 lb. avg. 10 to 12 oz.	Softball	2 to 2 ½ cups
Medium	6 to 9 oz. avg. 8 oz.	Baseball	1 to 1½ cups
Small	3½ to 6 oz. avg. 4½ oz.	Tennis ball	1 cup or less

for up to four months using this method, with less than ¼ bushel spoiling. Stored in the crisper section of the refrigerator, quinces will keep for weeks. But don't store quinces with other fruits. They hasten ripening, and the scent transfers.

Seasonal Eating

Autumn is my favorite time of year to cook. The harvest is abundant and varied. The recipes in this collection rely heavily on using quality in-season fruits and vegetables, at the peak of freshness.

Eating seasonally is how our mothers, grandmothers, and ancestors cooked and fed their families. The wisdom of eating simply prepared, fresh foods is hard to dispute.

About the Ingredients

Fresh quince refers to whole, ripe fruit; fuzz removed and washed.

Many recipes call for grated quince. By this I mean shredded like a carrot. I use the grating disc of a food processor, but you can do it by hand.

Some recipes call for fine-grain table salt and finely ground black pepper; others call for coarse salt and freshly ground coarse black pepper. Please follow the directions exactly; it does make a difference.

Because some of us no longer live in regions that provide clear, low-mineral water from the tap, I list water as an ingredient where it may affect taste.

Less is more when it comes to sugar content in modern foods. Many of my recipes may seem to call for a lot of sugar. Personally, I prefer savory dishes over sweet. Having said that, please try the dish as written. If it's too sweet for your taste, you can adjust the second time around.

Quince Basics

Poached Quince

makes about 4 cups poached quince, plus 3 cups poaching liquid

This recipe is the most important recipe in the collection. Often, if not always, when you are using quince as an ingredient in pies, cakes, and side dishes, it's necessary to poach the fruit first. Precooking evens out the cooking times and tenderness of quince when pairing it with other fruits, such as pears, apples, or cranberries.

Slowly poaching quince on the stove top in syrup takes more than an hour. There are other methods of precooking the fruit (microwaving, roasting, slow cooking); I've tried them all, but the old-fashioned, long simmer method on the stove top is the only process that develops the characteristic caramel color and full-bodied flavor of the fruit. Respect tradition; fall in love with the process, and you'll discover that quince is worth the wait.

For me, it doesn't get much better than a succulent yet firm, blush-rose colored, slightly sweet poached quince wedge flavored with a hint of cinnamon. Slices can be served with a couple of spoonfuls of poaching liquid on pancakes, French toast, or waffles for breakfast; as an ice cream topping; or as a simple, pretty blush fruit compote.

8 cups water

1 cup sugar

2 tablespoons fresh lemon juice (1 lemon)

One 3-inch cinnamon stick

2 pounds fresh quince, peeled, cored, quartered, and cut into ½-inch-thick wedges (about 7 cups)

1. Combine the water, sugar, lemon juice, cinnamon stick, and quince in a large heavy-bottomed pot and quickly bring to a boil, stirring to dissolve the sugar. Gently simmer uncovered, stirring occasionally, for 1¼ hours, or until the quince is tender. The fruit will turn golden, then a blush salmon-pink color. The fruit is done when it can be pierced easily with a knife. Discard the cinnamon stick. Cool to room temperature.

2. Poached quinces may be jarred in their poaching syrup, stored in an airtight container and chilled (in the refrigerator) for a week, or frozen.

Note: You can easily halve, double, triple, and even quadruple the recipe by adjusting the ingredient quantities. However, do not add another cinnamon stick unless you are working with about 4 pounds of fruit. When poaching greater quantities of fruit, increase the size of your pot or use more than one pot. There should be enough water so that the quince wedges tumble freely as they cook; otherwise the wedges tend to break, especially toward the end of the cooking process. This will result in fewer whole slices to use in dessert dishes that call for attractive, complete wedges. Often I poach a large amount of fruit. That way I have poached quince on hand for a nice variety of quince dishes.

SAVE THE POACHING LIQUID!

In most recipes that use poached quince, the fruit is drained of its poaching liquid. Don't toss this slightly sweet rose-colored nectar! Instead, save it and use it to make Quince Fruit Leather (page 117).

Simple Baked Quince

serves 4

In season, cooks across the traditional quince-growing region of the world—Armenia, Iran, Turkey, and neighboring countries—value baked quince as the quintessential finish to an evening meal. Variations abound, limited only by a chef's imagination and available ingredients. I offer this simple yet elegant recipe as a beginning.

2 medium or large fresh quinces
2 to 4 tablespoons (½ stick) butter
4 tablespoons firmly packed light brown sugar
Ground cinnamon
Ground nutmeg
4 tablespoons (¼ cup) coarsely chopped walnuts
¼ cup heavy cream, whipped cream, plain yogurt, mascarpone cheese, crème fraîche, or kaymak
(see Note)

1. Preheat the oven to 375°F.
2. Place the fruit in a roasting pan filled 1 inch deep with water. The water prevents the fruit from burning where it rests on the pan. Cover securely with foil. Bake in the middle of the oven for 1 hour; flip the quince and rotate the pan at least once during cooking to ensure even baking and prevent burn spots.
3. Remove from the oven and let stand until the fruit is cool enough to handle. With a sharp knife, halve each quince; core completely with a knife, melon baller, or peach pitter. Place each cored half, cut side up, on a square of foil large enough to enclose the half when folded. Score the softened flesh with a sharp knife. This will help the flavorings seep into the fruit during the second baking.
4. Fill each half with ½ to 1 tablespoon of the butter (depending on size), 1 tablespoon of the brown sugar, and a dash or two of cinnamon and nutmeg. Then fold the sides of the foil up and around the quince and seal.

5. Return the wrapped quince to the roasting pan (drained of water), cut side up, and bake for 45 minutes to 1 hour, or until the fruit is very tender. The baking time will vary depending on the size and quality of the fruit.

6. Remove the pan from the oven. Carefully open the foil pouch and set each half on a dessert dish. Top each half with 1 tablespoon of the walnuts and a generous spoonful of dairy topping. Serve immediately while still warm.

Note: In Turkey, baked quince is served topped with a heavy clotted cream called *kaymak*. In the United States, kaymak is imported from Lebanon, Syria, or Turkey and sold in the dairy section in most Middle Eastern groceries.

Candied Quince

makes 1 pint

The Chinese cherish candied quince especially at the New Year, believing that the quince represents luck and fortune. The Greeks, the Serbs, the Armenians, and others pool glistening red, candied wedges in heavy cream or yogurt and serve the combination in delicate saucers with coffee or tea to afternoon guests. Straying from tradition is a delectable adventure, too. Add a few small pieces to your favorite baking recipe, such as lemon muffins or scones.

For those new to cooking with quince, this recipe is an excellent starting point. Candied quince is very easy to make, is delicious any way you serve it, and lasts for months when chilled.

1 pound fresh quince, peeled, cored, and cut into 1-inch-thick wedges (about 3 cups)
3 cups sugar

1. Gently toss the quince wedges with the sugar in a large mixing bowl until covered.
2. Transfer to a large heavy-bottomed pot and cook over medium heat until the sugar melts completely and begins to bubble. Stir often so the fruit does not burn. Reduce the heat to low and cook, stirring occasionally, for approximately 1¼ hours, or until the fruit is covered with a rich red caramel-colored, thick, gooey syrup.
3. Ladle through a wide-mouthed funnel into sterilized half-pint jars. Process (see page 114), or simply cover with lids and screw tops and keep refrigerated. Chilled, Candied Quince will keep for months.

Quintessential Quince Paste

makes about 1 pound

It's called *dulce de membrillo* in Spain, *geleia de marmelo* in Portugal, *quince cheese* in the United Kingdom, and *quince candy* in France—whatever your preference, this treat has won the hearts of foodies around the world. It's easy to make, versatile to serve, and great to gift.

My version contains one-third the sugar called for in traditional recipes. Higher sugar content often results in a gummy sweet, more like candy than a spread. My paste is easy to slice, has a hint of lemon, and resonates with sun-ripened, harvest color. Like Goldilocks, I'm sure you'll think it's "just right."

STOVE-TOP METHOD

1¾ to 2 pounds fresh quince, peeled, cored, and diced (about 6 cups)

9 cups water

¼ cup fresh lemon juice (2 lemons)

Sugar

Confectioners' sugar

1. Coat an 8-inch square cake pan with nonstick cooking spray and set aside.
2. Combine the quince and water in a large heavy-bottomed pot. Bring to a boil, lower the heat, and simmer uncovered, stirring occasionally, for 1½ hours, or until the fruit is very tender. The secret to a smooth, translucent paste is to cook the fruit until it is as close as quince can come to being mushy.
3. Remove from the heat and cool for 10 minutes. Do not cool to room temperature; the fruit purées best when warm. Transfer the cooked fruit with juices into the bowl of a food processor. Add the lemon juice and purée until smooth. At this stage, it will look and smell a lot like applesauce.

4. Push the purée through a fine sieve into a mixing bowl to remove any remaining lumps of fruit, if desired. Omit this step if you don't mind a few fruit chunks in your spread. I consider it a bonus.

5. Measure (in cups) the quantity of purée as you return it to the heavy-bottomed pot. You should have approximately 3 cups purée. Add ⅓ cup sugar for every 1 cup purée (for example, if you have 3 cups purée, add 1 cup sugar). (If you want to make quince candy, add 1 cup sugar for every 1 cup purée.)

6. Cook over moderate heat, stirring constantly, for about 1 hour, or until the mixture reduces to a thick, stiff consistency that forms soft peaks and pulls away from the sides and the bottom of the pan when stirred. It's done when you can form a soft compact ball with your fingers that easily retains its shape.

7. Spread the paste evenly in the prepared pan. Cool to room temperature, loosely cover with plastic wrap, and leave overnight or until set, at least 8 hours. Turn the paste out of the pan, cut into squares, and place the squares on a wire rack to dry for another 2 hours.

8. Sift confectioners' sugar over the squares, then wrap them in waxed paper and store in an airtight container in the refrigerator or freezer. Quince paste freezes well.

9. Slice and serve with cheese. Many cheeses work well. Tapas bars throughout Spain often pair quince paste with slightly salty Manchego cheese. I especially like Stilton or the layered combination of two English cheeses—Stilton and savory Double Gloucester—called Huntsman cheese. Roasted almonds are a traditional complement.

OVEN METHOD

Preheat the oven to 375°F. Place the fresh whole quinces (1¾ to 2 pounds) in a baking pan filled 1 inch deep with water. Cover with foil and bake in the middle of the oven until the fruit is very tender throughout, about 2 hours. Flip the fruit and rotate the pan at least once during the cooking time. Remove. When cool enough to handle, peel, core, and quarter the fruit. Transfer the pulp to the bowl of a food processor. Add ½ cup water and ¼ cup lemon juice. Purée as instructed in Step 3. Finish as directed.

Cinnamon-Spiced Quince Paste with Walnuts

Now that you know how to make basic quince paste, don't stop there. Add a pinch of cinnamon and chopped walnuts for an extra-special treat.

1 pound Quintessential Quince Paste

¼ teaspoon ground cinnamon

¼ cup coarsely chopped walnuts

Prepare the quince paste as directed. Add the cinnamon in Step 5, when you add the sugar and begin the final cooking process. Fold in the walnuts 5 minutes before removing the paste from the heat. Finish as directed.

Medicinal Quince Seed Tea

makes 1 cup

In the days before penicillin, in the small Blackstone Valley mill town in Massachusetts where my immigrant grandparents and other Armenians settled, my grandmother earned a reputation as an herbal healer. My cousin and I, carrying baskets of herbs, seeds, roots, or homemade concoctions Grandma had brewed on the stove, would trail behind her to an Armenian home where someone was sick or injured. Grandma delivered dried quince seeds to people with sore throats or digestive upsets; she explained how to brew a tea and drink it. Those suffering from sore gums, swollen eyes, chapped lips, and minor burns and wounds were instructed to soak the seeds in boiling water to release the gummy emollient, and then to use it as a salve.

In many cultures around the world, quince seeds have been harvested from fresh quince, dried, and used to treat both internal and external ailments. Throughout early American history, gummy quince mucilage preceded Brylcreem as a hair-styling gel.

1 cup water
1 tablespoon dried quince seeds
1 tablespoon honey
Squeeze of fresh lemon juice

Combine the water and quince seeds in a small saucepan and bring to a boil. Lower the heat to a vigorous simmer and cook for 5 to 6 minutes to obtain a thick mucilage. Strain into a mug. Stir in the honey and lemon juice and drink warm.

Note: Often quince recipes instruct cooks to include a few seeds in the cooking process, explaining that the seeds help the fruit deepen in color. This is a culinary urban legend; the seeds have nothing to do with the chemical changes that cause the pulp's hue transition.

Appetite Teasers

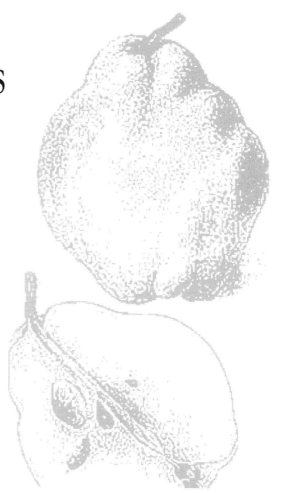

Quince-Orange Pickles

makes 3 pints

Grandma Kaprielian, an Armenian genocide survivor and matron of the Kaprielian family of greater Fresno, deserves credit for inspiring these scrumptious fruit pickles. Today, Grandma K's great nephew, John, is one of the largest commercial growers of quince in the United States.

I changed Grandma K's recipe a bit, but I'm sure she would approve! Chef John Karbowski, after his first bite, couldn't get enough of these pickles. He took a jar home to warm the appetites of his evening dinner guests—to rave reviews. Refrigerated, these sweet yet mouth-puckering quince and orange slices will keep for several months. Serve with thin slices of Manchego, Stilton, Asiago, goat, or aged cheddar cheese.

1¾ to 2 pounds fresh quince, peels left on, cored, and cut into ½-inch-thick wedges (about 7 cups)

1½ cups water

1 large orange, peel left on, cut across the middle as if preparing to squeeze it, seeds removed, and cut into ½-inch-thick triangle-shaped wedges

2 cups sugar

1 cup muscatel wine vinegar (see Note)

1 cup muscatel wine

One 3-inch cinnamon stick

6 whole cloves

1. Combine the quince slices and water in a large heavy-bottomed pot. Bring to a boil, lower the heat, and simmer until the quince turns golden and begins to soften, about 20 minutes. Drain through a sieve; reserve the cooked fruit and liquid separately. Set both aside.
2. Combine the orange slices, sugar, vinegar, wine, cinnamon stick, cloves, and ¾ cup reserved quince liquid in a large heavy-bottomed pot. Bring to a boil, stirring to dissolve the sugar, then lower the heat, cover, and simmer for 10 minutes.

3. Add the reserved quince slices. Cover and simmer for 20 minutes. Remove the cover and continue to simmer for an additional 20 minutes, or until just enough syrup remains to just cover the fruit when jarred. Discard the cinnamon stick and cloves.

4. Ladle through a wide-mouthed funnel into sterilized half-pint jars. Process (see page 114), or simply cover with lids and screw tops and keep refrigerated. Chilled, these pickles will outlast your appetite for eating them.

Note: Whole Foods Market offers a wide variety of vinegars, including muscatel wine vinegar. Please try not to substitute; using the correct vinegar makes these pickles truly delicious.

Simply Quince

Quince Salsa

makes 2 to 2½ cups

This mild salsa is one of the most tempting dishes in the collection. I actually suffer cravings for it. Break out the tortilla chips and serve it as a dipping sauce, a topper for fresh fish tacos, or off-the-grill salmon, swordfish, halibut, shrimp, or chicken.

½ to ¾ pound fresh quince, peeled, cored, and grated (2 to 2½ cups)

½ cup dry white wine

½ cup water

One 14¼-ounce can diced tomatoes, drained, mashed, and drained again to remove excess juices (about ½ cup packed pulp)

¼ cup finely diced or grated yellow onion

2 teaspoons grated jalapeño pepper

¼ cup finely chopped fresh cilantro

¾ teaspoon coarse salt

2 to 3 tablespoons fresh lime juice (1 to 2 limes)

1. Combine the grated quince, wine, and water in a medium-sized saucepan. Bring to a boil, lower the heat, and simmer until almost all the liquid is gone, 20 to 25 minutes. Cooking quince in dry white wine enhances the natural flavor of the fruit. Transfer the cooked quince to a mixing bowl.
2. Add the tomato pulp, onion, jalapeño, cilantro, salt, and 2 tablespoons of the lime juice and mix well. Add the remaining 1 tablespoon lime juice to taste, if necessary. Cover and chill for at least 30 minutes before serving. Best consumed the day it's made.

Open-Faced Quince Sandwiches with Arugula and Parmesan

serves 20

A favorite Arabic spread of mine, *muhammarah*, is a pomegranate-walnut mix spiced with cayenne.

One day, bursting with inspiration, curiosity, and hopeful enthusiasm, I charged into the kitchen to see if the concept could be adapted for quince. The successful results are offered here for your enjoyment.

for the quince:

1 pound fresh quince, poached according to the directions on page 27
(2 cups poached quince, drained and coarsely chopped)

for the sandwiches:

½ cup chopped yellow onion (1 small)
1 tablespoon extra-virgin olive oil, plus more for brushing
Pinch of cayenne
¼ teaspoon freshly ground black pepper
¾ teaspoon coarse salt
½ cup walnuts
1 baguette
1 bunch baby arugula, stems trimmed
1 cup shaved Parmigiano-Reggiano cheese

1. Prepare the quince as directed.
2. Sauté the onion in 1 tablespoon olive oil in a medium-sized skillet over medium heat until tender, about 6 minutes. Add the cayenne, black pepper, and salt; stir to

blend. Transfer to the bowl of a food processor. Add the quince and walnuts; pulse to a chunky paste. The spread can be made and refrigerated a few days ahead.

3. When ready to serve, cut the baguette into 12 long diagonal slices, each about 5 inches long and ½ inch thick. Lightly brush both sides of the slices with olive oil. Arrange the bread on a baking sheet and broil for about 1 minute on each side.

4. Spread the toasts with quince-walnut pâté; top each with arugula and cheese. Arrange on a platter and serve.

Curried Quince and Lamb Purses with Cilantro Yogurt Dipping Sauce

makes 40 to 90 pieces, depending on the size of the wrappers used

Once upon a time, my cousin Craig worked for a caterer who introduced him to the wonders of wonton wrappers. We have him to thank for these crisp mouthfuls.

At first glance this recipe may seem time and labor intensive, but the stuffing and the sauce can be made ahead and refrigerated; once stuffed, the bundles keep for up to 2 days, chilled, and they also freeze well. Cooking the delightful morsels is the only step required before your guests arrive.

for the stuffing:
¾ pound fresh quince, peeled, cored, and grated (about 2½ cups)

½ cup dry white wine

½ cup water

2 sweet onions, finely chopped

¼ cup extra-virgin olive oil

½ pound ground lamb

½ cup finely chopped fresh flat-leaf parsley

½ teaspoon curry powder

1½ teaspoons coarse salt

¼ teaspoon ground black pepper

for the sauce:
1 cup coarsely chopped fresh cilantro

½ jalapeño pepper, stem and seeds removed, quartered

½ teaspoon fresh lemon juice

1 cup plain yogurt

for the purses:
Wonton wrappers (about 40 squares; 90 rounds)
Vegetable oil

1. If possible, prepare the stuffing a few days ahead and refrigerate. If you decide to make the wontons the same day as serving them, the filling needs to cook and cool to room temperature before using, so plan accordingly.
2. Combine the grated quince, wine, and water in a small saucepan. Bring to a boil, lower the heat, and simmer until most of the liquid is gone, 20 to 25 minutes. Set aside.
3. In a large deep-sided saucepan, sauté the onions in the olive oil over medium-high heat until tender and translucent, about 10 minutes. Add the lamb, breaking the meat up into small pieces when adding. Stir frequently. Cook the meat until browned, 3 to 5 minutes. Add the quince with any remaining wine broth and the parsley, curry, salt, and black pepper. Lower the heat and cook very slowly until the mixture is not too wet or too dry, no more than 10 minutes. Set aside to cool to room temperature. Cover and chill in an airtight container, if desired.
4. To prepare the dipping sauce, combine the cilantro, jalapeño, lemon juice, and yogurt in the bowl of a food processor; pulse until smooth. The sauce will be a light green when done. Transfer to a bowl, cover, and chill until serving time.
5. Once the filling and dipping sauce are made, begin assembly. Set a bowl filled with water near a flat work surface. Wet the edges of each wrapper with a pastry brush or a fingertip dipped in water. Place less than 1 teaspoon of stuffing in the center. Fold the shell up and around the stuffing, like a flower bud. Gently press the moist edges together so they adhere to each other and close. Set the stuffed wonton on a plate in preparation for frying. Repeat until all wrappers are stuffed. Cover and refrigerate the bundles or freeze them for use later, if desired.
6. Fill a large heavy-bottomed pot 1 to 2 inches deep with vegetable oil and layer a large plate with paper towels for draining. Heat the oil over medium-high heat until it's very hot but not sizzling or spitting (375°F). Place a few wontons in the hot oil; leave room in the pot to fry each evenly. Fry golden brown and crispy, about 3 minutes. Remove with a slotted spoon and drain.
7. Serve immediately arranged on a pretty serving tray with the dipping sauce nearby.

Quince and Butternut Squash Soup with Curry

serves 8

This is a light, delicate soup with an appetizing golden-copper color. Eat hot or cold.

4 cups chicken broth
1 bay leaf, fresh if available
¾ pound fresh quince, peeled, cored, and cut into small cubes (about 2½ cups)
2½ pounds (1 small or medium) butternut squash, peeled, seeded, and cut into small cubes
1 large yellow onion, cut into chunks
2 tablespoons sugar
¾ teaspoon coarse salt
¾ teaspoon curry powder

for garnish, optional:
Shaved or shredded Parmigiano-Reggiano cheese
Plain yogurt and chopped fresh parsley

1. Combine the broth, bay leaf, quince, squash, and onion in a large heavy-bottomed pot. Cover and bring to a boil over medium-high heat. Lower the heat, stir in the sugar and salt, and simmer, covered, for 45 minutes or until the quince and squash chunks are very tender.
2. Remove from the heat, add the curry, and discard the bay leaf. Set aside 1½ cups of the cooked quince and squash to dice and add for garnish. Transfer the remaining mixture to the bowl of a food processor or blender and purée until smooth.
3. Garnish with the reserved diced quince and squash and your choice of optional garnishes, if using. If eating warm, reheat before serving.

Succulent Salads

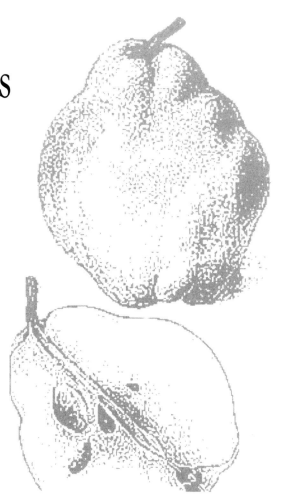

Quince-Infused Vinegar

makes about 1½ cups

Enjoy the distinctive flavor of quince on your salads year round. This fruit vinegar offers a mild, slightly sweet accent to tossed green salads, requiring only a dash of salt and a grind of black pepper to complete. When bottled, this deep blush-orange vinegar makes a great hostess gift.

For best results, chop, shred, or grate the raw fruit pulp fine to release the greatest amount of natural juices into the vinegar during the steeping process. Lemon thyme is an excellent accompaniment.

4 cups white wine vinegar
1 cup sugar
½ to ¾ pound fresh quince, peeled, cored, and grated (2 to 2½ cups)

1. Combine the vinegar, sugar, and quince in a medium-sized heavy-bottomed saucepan. Bring to a boil, stirring until the sugar is completely dissolved. Lower the heat to a gentle simmer and cook for 15 minutes. Make sure to provide proper ventilation to disperse the vinegar fumes.
2. Turn the heat off and let stand for 30 minutes.
3. Line a sieve with moistened, double-lined cheesecloth. Set the sieve over a bowl and strain the fruit-vinegar mixture. Discard the fruit and return the vinegar to the saucepan. At this stage in the process, the vinegar will be a golden-apricot color.
4. Reheat and boil gently for 15 minutes. This second boil reduces the vinegar to a rich orange color and intensifies the flavor. Pour into clean, sterilized glass bottles or jars with airtight lids and store in a cool dark place or in the refrigerator. This vinegar only improves with age.

Casaba Melon and Prosciutto Salad Dressed with Quince Vinegar

serves 4

Casaba melons and quinces both claim Persian origin as well as the distinction of having been cultivated for thousands of years. They have been likely flavor matches for centuries. The ripe melon's creamy-colored flesh is extremely juicy and has a mild cucumber-like flavor that plays well with salty prosciutto and the gentle nutty flavor of imported Gouda cheese. A drizzle of slightly sweet quince-steeped vinegar melds the different flavor notes together perfectly.

4 thin slices prosciutto di Parma
4 wedges of peeled and seeded ripe casaba melon (see Note)
2 ounces aged Danish Gouda cheese, curled
2 tablespoons Quince-Infused Vinegar (page 49)

Arrange a thin slice of prosciutto di Parma on a salad plate. Top with a melon wedge. Garnish with cheese curls and dress with quince vinegar. Serve immediately.

Note: Ripe honeydew melon easily substitutes for casaba. When serving honeydew, use Roquefort or Stilton cheese.

Watercress, Red Onion, and Quince Salad with Sweet Mustard Vinaigrette

serves 4

A member of the mustard family, wild watercress thrived in the gentle flow of the crisp, clear, waters of the brook behind my grandmother's garden in Massachusetts. A fruiting quince tree grew near the brook behind the house next door. Watercress and quince have been paired in my mind since childhood, and—with the creation of this salad—today they are paired on my table. The pine nuts add a buttery crunch that's nice, but not necessary. A lively Champagne or sparkling wine complements this salad to perfection.

for the quince:
½ pound fresh quince, poached according to the directions on page 27
(about eight ½-inch-thick wedges, drained)

for the salad:
4 cups watercress
¼ red onion, sliced paper thin
4 ounces aged goat cheese, cut into ¼-inch dice (¼ cup)
1 tablespoon toasted pine nuts, optional

for the dressing:
3 tablespoons extra-virgin olive oil
1½ tablespoons red wine vinegar
2 teaspoons Dijon mustard
½ teaspoon sugar
½ teaspoon coarse salt

1. Prepare the quince as directed.
2. Evenly divide and layer the watercress, onion, quince wedges, and cheese on individual salad plates.
3. Whisk the dressing ingredients together in a small bowl until well blended.
4. Drizzle the dressing evenly over each salad and sprinkle pine nuts on top, if using. Serve at once.

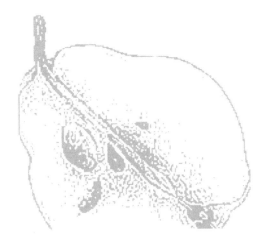

Grilled Chicken and Quince Cobb Salad with Roquefort

serves 4 to 6

Composed in a circle with salmon-pink quince at the center, this classic American salad is as eye-catching as it is flavorful; certainly hearty enough to be served as a meal.

for the quince:

½ pound fresh quince, poached according to the directions on page 27
(1 cup poached quince, drained and coarsely chopped)

for the salad:

¾ pound whole skinless chicken breast (about 1 breast), washed and patted dry

1 tablespoon olive oil

Coarse salt and freshly ground black pepper

Ground cumin

2 cups hand-torn Boston lettuce

1 cup hand-torn romaine lettuce

2 tomatoes, seeded and finely chopped

2 pickling or Persian cucumbers, peeled and diced

½ pound bacon, well-cooked, drained, and broken into large pieces

1 avocado, peeled and sliced

½ hard-cooked egg, shelled

¼ red onion, diced small, or 2 green onions, white and light green sections only, finely chopped

for the dressing (see Note):
¼ cup Quince-Infused Vinegar (page 49)
1 tablespoon extra-virgin olive oil
2 tablespoons finely grated Roquefort cheese (2 ounces)

1. Prepare the quince as directed.
2. Prepare the grill. Brush the chicken breast with olive oil. Sprinkle with salt, black pepper, and cumin to taste. Grill until tender, about 4 minutes per side. Cool slightly and dice fine.
3. Toss the lettuces together in a large bowl, then arrange over the surface of a large circular serving platter. Pile the chopped quince like a bull's-eye in the center. Radiating outward, arrange the tomatoes, cucumbers, bacon, and avocado in concentric circles around the quince center as if creating a dart board.
4. Finely grate the egg yolk and white. Combine the egg with the onion in a small bowl, tossing to mix. Avoiding the quince at the center, sprinkle the egg mixture evenly over the top of the salad.
5. Whisk the dressing ingredients together in a small bowl until well blended. Drizzle evenly over the entire salad, or serve on the side, if desired. Serve at room temperature.

Note: If you have not made Quince-Infused Vinegar, this dressing is a good substitute: ¼ cup extra-virgin olive oil, 1½ tablespoons red wine vinegar, ½ teaspoon dry mustard, and 2 tablespoons finely grated Roquefort cheese.

South-of-the-Border Shrimp Salad with Twice-Cooked Quince

serves 4 to 6

In the handsome city of Oaxaca, Mexico, street vendors sell raw quince slices drizzled with a hot pepper sauce. Although not tempted by this offering during my stay, I created this salad in honor of the quince's long-established prominence on the Latin table. Complete the celebration with a huge pitcher of margaritas or *cervezas bien frias* (well-chilled beers). *Salud!*

for the quince:
1 pound fresh quince, poached according to the directions on page 27
(about sixteen ½-inch-thick wedges, drained)

for the shrimp:
4 tablespoons (½ stick) butter
3 cloves garlic, crushed
1½ teaspoons ground cumin
¼ teaspoon cayenne
1 teaspoon coarse salt
¼ cup fresh lime juice (2 to 3 limes)
1 pound raw shrimp with tails

for the salad:
4 cups baby spinach
1 bunch watercress
1 bunch fresh cilantro, coarsely chopped
1 cup julienned jicama (see Note)

½ red onion, sliced thin
1 avocado, peeled and sliced

for the dressing:
¼ cup extra-virgin olive oil
⅓ cup fresh lime juice (3 to 4 limes)
½ teaspoon coarse salt
Freshly ground black pepper

1. Prepare the quince as directed.
2. Preheat the broiler.
3. To prepare the marinade, melt the butter in a small saucepan with the garlic, cumin, cayenne, salt, and ¼ cup lime juice.
4. Arrange the shrimp and quince wedges in a shallow broiling pan lined with foil. Spoon the marinade evenly over the top. Broil under high heat, rotating the pan and tossing once, until the shrimp are evenly cooked, about 6 to 8 minutes. Using a slotted spoon, remove the shrimp and quince wedges to separate dishes and set aside.
5. To prepare the salad, toss the spinach, watercress, cilantro, jicama, and onion together in a large salad bowl.
6. To prepare the dressing, combine the olive oil, ⅓ cup lime juice, salt, and 4 of the quince wedges in the bowl of a food processor or blender. Purée until smooth, then add black pepper to taste. Pour over the greens and toss to blend.
7. Arrange the greens on individual serving plates. Distribute the shrimp, remaining quince wedges, and avocado slices evenly among the plates. Serve at once while the shrimp and quince wedges are still warm. Accompany with toasted baguettes.

Note: A native of Latin America, jicama is a root vegetable with a thin brown skin and white, crunchy pulp. Peel just before using, then cut the sweet and juicy, chestnut-type textured flesh into thin matchsticks (julienned). Jicama is available year-round and can be purchased in Latin American markets and most supermarkets.

Heirloom Tomato and Quince Salad

serves 4

Once I discovered that quince and tomato proved heavenly together, ripe heirloom plum tomatoes at the farmers' market beckoned me to wed them with early-ripening pineapple quince. Feta cheese adds a touch of salt, and fresh mint finishes this cooling salad or crostini topping.

for the quince:
½ pound fresh quince, poached according to the directions on page 27
(1 cup poached quince, drained and diced)

for the salad:
1 pound heirloom tomatoes, cut into bite-sized pieces (about 3 cups)
2 tablespoons chopped fresh mint
¼ cup crumbled feta cheese
2 teaspoons extra-virgin olive oil
1 tablespoon fresh lime or lemon juice
Coarse salt and freshly ground black pepper

1. Prepare the quince as directed.
2. Combine the tomato and quince in a bowl. Toss in the mint and feta. Drizzle with olive oil and blend, then add the lime or lemon juice and sprinkle evenly with salt and black pepper. Toss to blend.
3. Serve with fresh, crusty bread as a side salad, or top crostini ("little toasts" brushed with olive oil) for a delicious hors d'oeuvre.

Quince, Pancetta, and White Kidney Bean Salad

serves 6

Poached quince is used as a light touch against salty pancetta and the sturdy, neutral backdrop of white kidney beans. Red pepper complements the sweetness of the fruit, and green onions add zip. Also delicious served on toasted baguettes as an appetizer.

for the quince:

½ pound fresh quince, poached according to the directions on page 27
(1 cup poached quince, drained and diced)

for the salad:

4 ounces pancetta, diced small (⅓ cup cooked) (see Note)
Two 15-ounce cans white kidney beans, washed and drained
½ red bell pepper, diced small (about ½ cup)
¼ cup finely chopped fresh flat-leaf parsley
3 green onions, white and light green sections only, finely chopped (about 2 tablespoons)

for the dressing:

¼ cup extra-virgin olive oil
¼ cup fresh lemon juice (2 lemons)
¾ teaspoon coarse salt
¼ teaspoon freshly ground black pepper
Smidgen of cayenne

1. Prepare the quince as directed.
2. Cook the pancetta in a skillet over medium heat, stirring frequently, until soft and tender with most of the fat rendered, about 10 minutes. Drain on paper towels.
3. Toss the pancetta, beans, red pepper, parsley, onions, and quince together in a large mixing bowl.
4. Whisk the dressing ingredients together in a small bowl until well blended. Pour over the salad and toss to blend.
5. Serve slightly chilled with a generous portion of pita slices.

Note: Trader Joe's sells a 4-ounce package of diced pancetta that is perfect for use in this recipe.

Sensational Sides

Quince-Apple Sauce

makes 4 cups

Applesauce reigns supreme in the United States. No longer! This quince-apple blend's golden-pink blush is warmer and more appetizing than traditional applesauce. It offers a greater depth of flavor, too. Maybe the best thing about cooking up a batch is the rich and heady perfume, suggestive of a mix of narcissus, apples, and pears, that will permeate your kitchen during the process. Smooth or chunky, the texture is up to you.

Serve as a companion to pork roast, alongside roasted sweet potato fries, mixed with cottage cheese as a midday treat, or on pancakes for breakfast. Once you try it, there will be no going back. Double the recipe and make a big batch. It freezes well.

¾ cup apple cider or unsweetened juice, plus more to thin

One 1 × 3-inch strip lemon rind

¼ cup fresh lemon juice (2 lemons)

One 3-inch cinnamon stick

¼ cup sugar plus ¼ cup, depending on taste

2 pounds fresh quince, peeled, cored, and grated (about 7 cups)

2 firm, juicy apples (Fuji, Braeburn, or Pink Lady apples; see Note), peeled, cored, and diced (about 3 cups)

1. Combine the apple cider or juice, lemon rind, lemon juice, cinnamon stick, ¼ cup of the sugar, and quince in a large heavy-bottomed pot. Cover and quickly bring to a boil over high heat. Stir often to ensure even cooking. Lower the heat and simmer very gently, covered, for 20 minutes; continue to stir often.
2. Add the apples. Quickly return to a boil, then lower the heat to a simmer and cook, covered, for another 30 minutes, stirring frequently so the fruit doesn't burn. Discard the lemon rind and cinnamon stick. Use a potato masher to mash and stir the sauce, alternately, until the consistency matches your preference. If a smooth loose texture is desired, transfer to the bowl of a food processor and pulse until

smooth. Add additional apple cider or juice, 1 tablespoon at a time, until you reach the preferred consistency.

3. Taste for sweetness. Most palates will judge the sauce too tart at this stage; add 1 tablespoon sugar at a time up to an additional ¼ cup, if desired.

4. Serve warm or at room temperature. Transfer any unused portion to an airtight container. Keeps fresh for about a week in the refrigerator and freezes well.

Note: The Golden Delicious apple is the traditional apple used to make applesauce. However, the Fuji, Braeburn, and Pink Lady apple varieties have more juice than Goldens, making them a better match with quince with regard to cooking time, while also complementing quince's lower water content.

Quince-Cranberry Sauce

serves 8

Don't be deceived by the simplicity of this holiday alternative to traditional cranberry sauce. The just-cooked red cranberries paint an eye-catching, flavor-popping mosaic on your golden-orange canvas of mild-flavored quince. Each bite explodes with flavor.

1½ pounds fresh quince, peeled, cored, and diced (3 cups)

2 cups water

¼ cup fresh orange juice

2 teaspoons orange zest

2 whole cloves

½ cup sugar plus ¼ cup, depending on taste

½ teaspoon coarse salt

1 cup fresh or frozen whole cranberries

1. Combine the quince, water, orange juice, orange zest, cloves, and ¼ cup of the sugar in a large heavy-bottomed pot; toss to mix. Bring to a boil, stirring until the sugar dissolves. Lower the heat and simmer, stirring occasionally, until the quince chunks are soft and tender, about 45 minutes.
2. Remove from the heat. Discard the cloves; while the mixture is still warm, mash with a potato masher. At this stage, the mixture will resemble a chunky, golden-orange-colored applesauce. Add the remaining ¼ cup sugar and salt and stir until the sugar dissolves completely. Add the cranberries.
3. Return the pot to the stove and continue cooking over medium-high heat, stirring until the berries pop, 3 to 5 minutes. Remove from the heat and taste. Adjust the sweetness by adding 1 tablespoon sugar at a time up to an additional ¼ cup, if desired.
4. Delicious when served with roasted turkey or pork. Store in an airtight container. Refrigerated, it will keep about a week. Or freeze it; it freezes well.

Grilled Polenta and Portobello Mushrooms with Balsamic Quince

serves 8 to 10

This hearty side has it all—crisp polenta, earthy mushrooms, succulent quince, and savory herbs. Better yet, it easily transforms into a busy-weeknight meal. Vegetarians lusting for a new taste will savor the robust combination of flavors and textures on a bed of mixed greens as a main course. If you are not vegetarian, keep the grill stoked. Lamb rib or loin chops grill up quickly, 3 to 4 minutes per side. Quince and lamb have been friends forever.

for the quince:

¾ pound fresh quince, poached according to the directions on page 27
(about twelve ½-inch-thick wedges, drained)

for the marinade:

¼ cup extra-virgin olive oil, plus more for brushing

⅓ cup balsamic vinegar

2 cloves garlic, minced

2 tablespoons chopped fresh flat-leaf parsley

1 teaspoon chopped fresh thyme

1 teaspoon chopped fresh oregano

1 teaspoon coarse salt

¼ teaspoon freshly ground black pepper

for the dish:

6 portobello mushrooms, stems and caps separated, halved if very large

1 pound set cooked polenta, cut into twelve ½-inch-thick rounds

½ cup low-sodium vegetable or chicken broth

1 tablespoon butter

8 cups baby mixed greens, optional

1 tablespoon shaved Parmigiano-Reggiano cheese

1. Prepare the quince as directed.
2. To prepare the marinade, combine ¼ cup of the olive oil and the balsamic vinegar, garlic, parsley, thyme, oregano, salt, and black pepper in a nonreactive bowl. Add the mushrooms and toss to cover. Let stand for 1 hour, tossing occasionally. When ready to prepare the dish, transfer the mushrooms to a plate and set aside. Reserve the marinade for later.
3. Preheat the grill to medium-high. Lightly brush the tops and bottoms of the polenta rounds with olive oil. Cook the rounds on the grill until crisp, flipping once, 6 to 8 minutes per side. (The trick to grilling polenta is to know when to flip it. Wait until the entire piece can be lifted off the grates cleanly with a metal spatula. This way, the crisp surface won't stick to the grill and tear away in spots.) Set the grilled rounds aside on a plate.
4. Place the mushrooms on a cooler part of the grill and cook, turning often to avoid burning, until tender, about 10 minutes. Set aside on a plate.
5. Pour the reserved marinade into a medium-sized saucepan. Bring to a boil, then lower the heat and simmer for about 1 minute. Add the broth, boil again, then lower the heat and simmer until reduced by half (⅓ to ½ cup), about 10 minutes. Remove from the stove top and stir in the butter until melted. Add the quince wedges, tossing to cover.
6. Arrange the polenta, mushrooms, and quince slices on a large serving plate (over the greens, if using). Drizzle half of the reduced marinade evenly over the top and garnish with cheese. Serve immediately, with extra marinade on the side.

Cumin-Glazed Carrots and Quince

serves 8

Tangy and sweet, this simple root-fruit combo is a savory complement to poultry, pork, and lamb.

¾ pound baby carrots, cut into bite-sized pieces (about 2½ cups)

½ pound fresh quince, peeled, cored, and diced (1 to 1½ cups)

1 tablespoon olive oil

2 tablespoons butter

1½ cups water

2 tablespoons fresh lemon juice (1 lemon)

1 tablespoon honey

½ teaspoon ground cumin

½ teaspoon coarse salt

¼ teaspoon freshly ground black pepper

1. Combine the carrots, quince, olive oil, and butter in a heavy-bottomed saucepan and sauté over medium heat, stirring constantly, until well coated, about 2 minutes.
2. Add the water, lemon juice, honey, cumin, salt, and pepper and simmer, uncovered and stirring occasionally, until the liquid is evaporated and the carrots and quince are tender and glazed, about 40 minutes. Serve warm.

Simply Quince

Creamy Cauliflower-Quince Gratin

serves 8 to 10

Last fall, my cousin saw this dish on the menu of an upscale Philadelphia restaurant. He didn't order it, but the concept intrigued him. A week or so later, with my help on how to prepare the quince, he cobbled together the basics of this recipe and brought the dish to a Thanksgiving gathering. Everyone loved it. With many thanks to that unknown Philadelphia chef for his inspiration and cousin Craig for his adventurous culinary spirit, you, too, can bring it to your holiday gathering and enjoy the praise.

for the quince:
½ to ¾ pound fresh quince, poached according to the directions on page 27
(1 to 1½ cups poached quince, drained and diced)

for the casserole:
4 tablespoons (½ stick) butter
1 head white cauliflower, washed and cut into florets
½ cup finely diced shallots (about 3)
1 tablespoon olive oil
1 tablespoon white all-purpose flour
1 cup heavy cream
¼ teaspoon salt
¼ teaspoon ground black pepper
Pinch of cayenne
1 clove garlic, crushed
1 teaspoon chopped fresh rosemary
1 cup grated Asiago cheese
1 tablespoon lemon zest
¼ cup plain bread crumbs
¼ cup grated Parmigiano-Reggiano cheese

1. Prepare the quince as directed.
2. Preheat the oven to 350°F. Grease a 9 × 9-inch square baking pan with 1 tablespoon of the butter and set aside.
3. Bring a large pot of salted water to a boil, add the cauliflower and cook the florets until partially softened, about 5 minutes. Drain immediately and set aside in a large mixing bowl.
4. Sauté the shallots in the olive oil over medium heat until golden and slightly browned, about 8 minutes. Add the shallots and quince to the cauliflower and toss to mix.
5. Whisk together the flour and 2 tablespoons of the butter in a small heavy-bottomed saucepan over medium heat until they combine into a smooth paste. Add the cream and cook, stirring, until the mixture thickens into a cream sauce, 3 to 5 minutes. Stir in the salt, black pepper, cayenne, garlic, and rosemary. Pour the cream mixture over the cauliflower mixture. Fold in the Asiago and lemon zest. Spoon the mixture into the prepared pan.
6. Combine the bread crumbs and Parmigiano-Reggiano in a small bowl, then sprinkle evenly over the top of the cauliflower. Dot the top with the remaining 1 tablespoon butter. Bake uncovered in the middle of the oven for 40 minutes. Remove when the juices are nice and bubbly and the top is golden brown.

Mashed Yams and Quince with Ginger and Cardamom

serves 8 to 10

Whipped yams pop with surprise bits of zesty quince. This side complements grilled turkey or chicken beautifully. The dish is an adaptation of a recipe I found in Aliza Green's tome *Starting with Ingredients*. Thank you, Aliza, for the wonderful idea!

¾ pound fresh quince, peeled, cored, and diced (about 2 cups)

2½ cups water

1¾ pounds (3 to 4) yams, peeled and cut into ½-inch chunks

2 tablespoons honey

2 tablespoons grated or chopped peeled fresh ginger

½ teaspoon ground cardamom

3 tablespoons unsalted butter, cubed

½ teaspoon coarse salt

Freshly ground black pepper

1. Simmer the quince in the water over medium heat, uncovered, until the fruit is tender, 35 to 40 minutes. (Begin step 2 after 15 minutes.) Remove from the heat without draining.
2. When the quince has been simmering for 15 minutes, set a collapsible vegetable steamer in a large saucepan, add 1 inch of water, cover, and bring to a boil. Add the yams and steam until soft, 20 to 25 minutes.
3. Combine the honey, ginger, and cardamom in a small bowl. Set aside.
4. When the yams are done, transfer them to the bowl of a food processor; add half of the cooked quince and liquid, the honey mixture, and the butter and salt. Pulse until smooth.

5. Turn into a serving bowl and fold in the remaining quince and liquid. Season with black pepper and serve immediately.

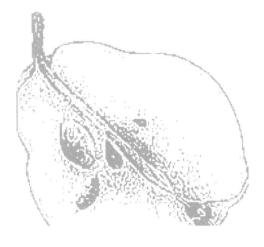

Simply Quince

Quince and Roasted Cashew Dressing

serves 12

This dish juxtaposes the slightly sweet flavor of tender quince with the buttery-rich crunch of toasted cashews to create a heavenly holiday dressing. Make it once and it just may become a family holiday tradition.

for the quince:

½ pound fresh quince, poached according to the directions on page 27

(1 cup poached quince, drained and coarsely chopped)

for the dressing:

5 tablespoons unsalted butter, plus more to grease the pan

1 loaf white country bread, crusts removed and cut into ½-inch pieces (about 7 cups)

½ pound ground pork

1 large yellow onion, chopped (1½ cups)

2 tablespoons olive oil

2½ celery stalks, finely chopped (1½ cups)

½ teaspoon salt

½ teaspoon ground black pepper

1 cup chopped fresh flat-leaf parsley

2 teaspoons dried oregano

One 14½-ounce can chicken broth

1 cup coarsely chopped toasted cashews (see Note)

1. Prepare the quince as directed.
2. Preheat the oven to 350°F. Coat a 9 × 13-inch baking dish with butter and set aside.
3. Melt 3 tablespoons of the butter in a large pot. Add the bread cubes and toss to cover. Spread the buttered cubes in a single layer on a rimmed baking sheet.

Toast in the oven, tossing once, until golden, 12 to 15 minutes. Remove and allow to cool completely.

4. Cook the pork in a medium-sized deep-sided skillet over medium heat, stirring often, until cooked yet slightly pink, about 5 minutes. Remove with a slotted spoon and drain on a bed of paper towels.

5. Wipe the skillet clean. Sauté the onion in the olive oil and 1 tablespoon of the butter over medium heat until softened, about 5 minutes. Add the celery, salt, and black pepper and cook, stirring occasionally, until the celery softens, about 8 minutes.

6. Transfer the onion mixture to a large mixing bowl. Stir in the parsley and oregano. Add the drained pork, cooled bread cubes, quince, broth, and cashews. Toss gently to mix.

7. Fill the prepared pan with dressing; scatter the remaining 1 tablespoon butter, cut into small cubes, over the top, and bake uncovered in the middle of the oven for about 45 minutes, or until golden brown on top. Serve warm. This dressing freezes well.

Note: Roast whole raw cashews in a single layer at 350°F for about 10 minutes, tossing once halfway through the cooking time. Cool completely before chopping.

Robust Stews

Lamb and Quince Tagine

serves 8

Tagines are savory Moroccan stews commonly served with couscous. They combine meat with vegetables, fruit, or both and are boldly spiced. The name refers to the earthenware vessel in which they are cooked.

From Northern Africa to Persia, there are as many versions of this stew as there are cooks. Finally, after many attempts, my cousin Craig and I developed our own version of this savory-sweet classic to mouthwatering perfection. I'm delighted and proud to share it with you, with blessings for great eating. As Craig says, "This stew is addictive!" A pinot noir with herbaceous qualities complements it beautifully.

1 large yellow onion, chopped

¼ cup olive oil

½ teaspoon ground cinnamon

¼ teaspoon ground allspice

¼ teaspoon ground cloves

½ teaspoon turmeric

Pinch of cayenne

¼ cup tomato paste

2 pounds boneless lamb, fat trimmed, cut into 1-inch squares

1 teaspoon salt

½ teaspoon ground black pepper

One 14½-ounce can peeled, diced tomatoes

3 cups water

1 pound fresh quince, peels left on, cored, and cut into bite-sized pieces (about 2 cups)

½ cup sugar

¼ cup red lentils, washed and picked of debris

Juice of 1 lemon

Chopped fresh flat-leaf parsley

1. Sauté the onion in the olive oil in a large heavy-bottomed pot over medium heat until tender and golden, about 8 minutes.
2. Lower the heat and stir in the cinnamon, allspice, cloves, turmeric, and cayenne. Add just a pinch of cayenne at this stage in the recipe: you can always add more later. Stir in the tomato paste and mix thoroughly; then add the lamb, salt, black pepper, and tomatoes. Raise the heat to medium-high and allow the mixture to bubble for about 5 minutes, stirring occasionally.
3. Add the water, bring the stew back to a boil, and then lower the heat, cover, and simmer for 30 minutes.
4. Add the quince, sugar, lentils, and lemon juice. Mix well. Simmer for another 30 minutes, or until the meat and quince pieces are tender and the sauce has thickened. Adjust the sugar and seasonings to taste.
5. Serve hot over a bed of pilaf, couscous, basmati rice, or mashed potatoes garnished with fresh parsley. Also delicious served with a wedge of hard cheese such as Manchego and a chunk of hearty bread.

Spicy Bay Scallops and Shrimp with Quince and Raisins

serves 8

This main-course stew stands unique in this collection, because from start to finish it comes together in about half an hour—record time for a quince dish. The recipe shows that quick-cooking fresh quince in the microwave can work well as long as the color of the fruit is not important to the dish. Celebrate the short prep time, and stealthy fire, of this seafood medley with a nice chardonnay or crisp sauvignon blanc.

for the quince:
1 pound fresh quince, poached according to the directions on page 27, or
microwaved according to the directions below (about sixteen ½-inch-thick wedges,
drained, reserving ½ cup poaching liquid)
2 cups water
½ cup sugar
1 tablespoon fresh lemon juice
One 3-inch cinnamon stick

for the seafood:
1 pound bay scallops
1 pound raw shrimp, shelled
1 teaspoon coarse salt
¼ teaspoon ground black pepper
1 teaspoon ground cumin
1½ cups small white cauliflower florets, washed
¾ cup raisins
1 yellow onion, chopped fine

2 cloves garlic, crushed

2 tablespoons extra-virgin olive oil

One 14½-ounce can diced tomatoes

2 tablespoons tomato paste

1½ teaspoons Aleppo pepper (no substitutions)

½ cup water

Chopped fresh flat-leaf parsley

1. Prepare the quince as directed on page 27. If microwaving, combine the water, sugar, lemon juice, and cinnamon stick in a large glass dish. Cover loosely and cook on high for 5 minutes. Stir until the sugar is fully dissolved before adding the quince. Cook on high, uncovered, for 10 minutes, stirring halfway through the cooking time. Check tenderness. Depending on your microwave, it may be necessary to heat for a few more minutes. Discard the cinnamon stick and drain, reserving ½ cup poaching liquid.
2. Toss the scallops and shrimp with the salt, black pepper, and cumin in a large mixing bowl and set aside.
3. Bring a large pot of salted water to a boil, add the cauliflower, and cook until partially softened, about 5 minutes. Drain immediately. Add the cauliflower to the seafood; toss and set aside.
4. In a small bowl, soak the raisins in just enough warm water to cover; set aside.
5. In a large heavy-bottomed pot, sauté the onion and garlic in the olive oil over medium heat until tender, about 8 minutes. Stir in the tomatoes, tomato paste, and Aleppo pepper. Mash smooth with a potato masher. Add the water, ½ cup of the reserved poaching liquid, and the quince to the pot. Simmer uncovered, stirring occasionally, for 10 minutes, or until the sauce thickens.
6. Add the seafood-cauliflower mixture and plumped raisins. Continue to simmer, stirring occasionally, until the seafood is cooked tender, about 8 minutes. Be careful not to overcook the seafood or it will toughen.
7. Serve immediately over couscous garnished with chopped fresh parsley.

Quintessential Quince Paste (page 32) and Cinnamon-Spiced Quince Paste with Walnuts (page 34)

Grilled Polenta and Portobello Mushrooms with Balsamic Quince (page 66)

Spicy Bay Scallops and Shrimp with Quince and Raisins (page 79)

Roast Pork Tenderloin with Quince and Root Vegetables (page 91)

Lamb-Stuffed Quince Dolmas (page 93)

Front to back: Fresh Ginger and Quince Pomegranate Chutney (page 107)
Quick Quince Chutney (page 109) and Quince and Red Pepper Chutney (page 105)

Quince-Cranberry-Walnut Conserve (page 122)
Fiery Quince-Tomato Spread (page 113) and Poached Quince (page 27)

Quince and Spiced Asian Pear Compote with Pomegranate, Yogurt, and Mint (page 133)

Classic Quince-Apple Jelly (page 129) and Scones with Quince (page 161)

Buttery Almond-Quince Phyllo Tarts (page 154)

Katayif Pastry Stuffed with Quince and Mascarpone Cheese (page 165)
and Quince-Infused Grappa (page 183)

White Pizza with Quince, Prosciutto, Asiago Cheese, and Chives (page 176)

Veal Shanks with Prunes, Apricots, and Quince

serves 8

Quince is popular in meat dishes in the Middle East and North Africa, but this stew seems more European to me, relying on veal rather than beef. The prunes and apricots fall apart during cooking and become the base for a rich, mustard-colored sauce.

I like to serve a pinot noir, especially one from Oregon, where the cool climate produces selections regarded for their ripe plum and cherry flavors. If you prefer white, a good Riesling will be your go-to wine with this dish.

1 large yellow onion, diced

2 tablespoons butter

1 tablespoon tomato paste

4 veal shank cross-cuts, also known as osso buco (about 2½ pounds)

Coarse salt and freshly ground black pepper

1½ cups water

½ teaspoon ground cumin

½ teaspoon ground cinnamon

½ teaspoon turmeric

⅛ to ¼ teaspoon cayenne

½ pound fresh quince, peel left on, cored, and cut into bite-sized pieces (1 to 1½ cups)

10 pitted prunes, cut into quarters

10 unsulfured dried apricots, cut into quarters

Chopped fresh mint, parsley, or cilantro, optional

Plain yogurt, optional

1. In a large heavy-bottomed pot, sauté the onion in the butter over medium heat until tender and lightly golden, about 8 minutes. Add the tomato paste and mix well.
2. Season the veal on both sides generously with salt and black pepper, place them in the pot, and sear on each side for 2 minutes. Add the water, cumin, cinnamon, turmeric, and ⅛ teaspoon of the cayenne. Blend well, then add the quince, prunes, and apricots.
3. Simmer for 2 hours, stirring occasionally, until the veal is fall-off-the-bone tender and the stew juices have thickened. Add the remaining ⅛ teaspoon cayenne, if desired. Discard the shank bones.
4. Garnish with your choice of chopped fresh herbs and a dollop of yogurt, if using, and serve over a bed of rice, bulgur pilaf, or couscous accompanied with a simple tossed green salad. Enjoy!

Chicken and Quince Stew

serves 8

This stew is a delicious one-pot dinner for a winter night. Smoked paprika is the secret ingredient.

It's a wonderful choice for entertaining; cook it a few days in advance, refrigerate, and reheat at serving time.

3 cloves garlic, minced

3 tablespoons olive oil

1 large yellow onion, quartered and sliced

1 small red bell pepper, chopped (about 1 cup)

½ pound fresh quince, peeled, cored, and cut into bite-sized pieces (1 to 1½ cups)

¼ cup raisins

2 cups chicken broth

1 teaspoon ground cumin

1 teaspoon smoked paprika

½ teaspoon ground coriander

½ teaspoon turmeric

¼ teaspoon ground cinnamon

1 teaspoon salt

½ teaspoon ground black pepper

1½ pounds boneless, skinless chicken breast, cut into bite-sized pieces

¼ cup chopped fresh flat-leaf parsley

3 tablespoons pistachio nuts, optional

1. Combine the garlic and olive oil in a large heavy-bottomed pot and sauté over medium heat until golden, about 3 minutes. Stir in the onion and continue to sauté until tender, about 5 minutes. Add the red pepper and cook for 3 minutes, until softened.

2. Add the quince, raisins, broth, cumin, paprika, coriander, turmeric, cinnamon, salt, and black pepper; stir well to mix. Cover, lower to medium heat, and cook at a gentle simmer for 40 minutes, or until the quince pieces are tender.

3. Stir in the chicken, cover, and simmer for 8 to 10 minutes, until the chicken is tender but cooked through.

4. Serve hot over couscous, pilaf, or rice and garnish with parsley and pistachios, if using. If you don't have time to prepare a side, the stew is very nice when served with crusty bread.

Turkey Chili with Quince

serves 8

This warmly spiced, mildly sweet chili is one of the most versatile dishes in the collection. Serve it as a casual dinner with crusty bread or spoon it over a toasted hamburger bun like a Sloppy Joe. Pile it on a tortilla and top with lettuce, tomatoes, onions, shredded cheese, and jalapeños to build a taco. Fill prebaked mini phyllo shells and serve them as warm appetizers to party guests. The flavor combinations are divine when paired with a dry sparkling wine.

¼ cup olive oil

2 yellow onions, diced

1 clove garlic, minced

1 tablespoon finely chopped peeled fresh ginger

½ teaspoon crushed red pepper flakes

¼ teaspoon ground allspice

¼ teaspoon ground cloves

⅓ cup tomato paste

1 teaspoon sugar

Two 14½-ounce cans peeled, diced tomatoes

¼ cup chopped fresh flat-leaf parsley

1 teaspoon salt

½ teaspoon freshly ground black pepper

½ to ¾ pound fresh quince, peel left on, cored, and cut into bite-sized pieces (1½ to 2 cups)

1¼ to 1½ pounds ground turkey

1. In a large heavy-bottomed pot, combine the olive oil, onions, and garlic. Sauté over medium heat, stirring occasionally, until the onions and garlic are tender and golden, about 10 minutes. Lower the heat to medium-low and add the ginger, red pepper flakes, allspice, and cloves. Cook, stirring, for 2 minutes, then add the tomato

paste and sugar and blend well. Add the tomatoes, parsley, salt, and black pepper. Simmer for 10 minutes. This will allow the liquid to cook down slightly.

2. Add the quince and turkey; break the meat up with your fingers while adding. Cover and simmer for 45 minutes, stirring occasionally. Remove the cover and cook for an additional 10 minutes, or until the liquid is reduced and the chili is thick and chunky.

Vegetarian Quince and Parsnip Medley

serves 8

The parsnip, like quince, couldn't be less glamorous. It's a cousin to the carrot, but it lacks its cousin's appealing orange hue; instead, the parsnip is a soft cream color. Like quince, the parsnip wasn't always so lowly. In the days when sweetness was dear, the saccharine root was a favored fall staple throughout medieval Europe. Then the potato came along, sugar got cheaper, and the parsnip went into gradual decline.

Given the parallels in their culinary histories, I couldn't resist pairing the ugly-duckling vegetable with the ugly-duckling fruit, and I'm so glad I did. When you combine them in this hearty vegetarian stew, you may change your mind about both. This curiously sweet stew is one of my daughter's favorites. She takes it to school and eats it cold for lunch.

1 large yellow onion, chopped

¼ cup extra-virgin olive oil

Two 14½-ounce cans diced tomatoes

1 teaspoon curry powder

½ teaspoon ground cinnamon

2 teaspoons coarse salt

½ teaspoon ground black pepper

½ teaspoon crushed red pepper flakes

1 pound parsnips, cut into bite-sized pieces (about 2 cups) (see Note)

½ to ¾ pound fresh quince, peel left on, cored, and cut into bite-sized pieces (1½ to 2 cups)

One 14- to 15-ounce can chickpeas, drained (also known as garbanzo beans)

½ cup chopped fresh flat-leaf parsley (about 1 bunch)

½ cup currants

1 cup vegetable broth

3 tablespoons pistachio nuts, optional

1. Sauté the onion in the olive oil in a large heavy-bottomed pot over medium heat until the onion begins to brown, 8 to 10 minutes. Add the tomatoes, curry, cinnamon, salt, black pepper, and red pepper flakes. Simmer, stirring occasionally, for about 5 minutes. Add the parsnips, quince, chickpeas, parsley, currants, and broth.
2. Cover and simmer, stirring occasionally, for 1¼ hours, or until the parsnips and quince are tender throughout. Adjust seasonings to taste.
3. Serve this hearty stew warm over a bed of bulgur pilaf, rich fluffy couscous, or rice. Sprinkle pistachio nuts on top, if you like a crunch.

Note: Buy firm parsnips. They should last up to 1 month when wrapped in a paper towel, placed in a plastic bag, and stored in the coldest section of your refrigerator. To prepare them, trim the ends and just skim off a very thin layer of the surface with a swivel-bladed peeler as you would with a carrot. (Peel completely, if waxed.) If the thicker end has a hard, woody core, remove it before chunking.

Main Dishes

Roast Pork Tenderloin with Quince and Root Vegetables

serves 6

Quince marmalades complement pork especially well. In this recipe the tangy-sweet quince spread plays a dual role—glazing both the meat and the winter vegetables. This dish is a fabulous choice for your family's wintertime Sunday meal.

for the pork:

1 boneless pork tenderloin (about 2½ pounds)

Coarse salt and freshly ground black pepper

½ pound fresh quince, peeled, cored, and cut into bite-sized pieces (1 to 1½ cups)

½ to 1 pound butternut squash, peeled, seeds removed, and cut into bite-sized pieces (about 1 to 1½ cups)

1 pound yams, peeled and cut into bite-sized pieces (about 3 cups)

1 large yellow onion, cut into chunks

2 tablespoons olive oil

Sprigs of fresh lemon thyme

for the glaze:

1½ cups Quince Marmalade (page 119; substitute orange marmalade if necessary)

1 tablespoon Dijon mustard

1 clove garlic, crushed

1. Preheat the oven to 350°F. Line a 9 × 13-inch baking pan with foil.
2. Season the pork with salt and black pepper. Set aside on a V-rack in a roasting pan.
3. In a large mixing bowl, combine the quince, squash, yams, and onion. Salt and pepper lightly. Add the olive oil and ½ cup of the marmalade; toss to mix.

4. Transfer three-quarters of the seasoned yam mixture to the bottom of the roasting pan. Set the rack with the pork on top in the center of the pan. Arrange the remaining yam mixture around the meat.

5. To prepare the glaze, combine the remaining 1 cup marmalade, mustard, and garlic in a small bowl. Spread evenly over the pork. Insert a meat thermometer in the pork, if using.

6. Cover the pan with foil. Roast in the middle of the oven for 1 hour; remove the cover and continue to roast for another 15 minutes, or until a thermometer registers 150°F.

7. Remove the thermometer, change the oven setting to broil, and broil for 5 minutes to brown the top. Transfer the roast to a cutting board and tent it with foil to keep it warm. Let it rest for 10 minutes before carving. (The internal temperature will rise as the pork rests.)

8. Drain the quince and vegetables of excess juices. While the roast is resting, return the pan with the fruit and vegetables to the oven and broil, stirring occasionally, until nicely browned, about 5 minutes.

9. For an elegant presentation, place the sliced pork in the center of a serving platter, surround the meat with the quince and vegetables, and garnish the dish with fresh lemon thyme.

Lamb-Stuffed Quince Dolmas

serves 4

The marriage of meat and vegetables and fruits during preparation is commonplace in Middle Eastern cuisine. Armenians, like most peoples of the Middle East and Mediterranean, stuff everything—vegetables such as peppers, squashes, and eggplants; leaves such as grape, Swiss chard, and collard greens; and fruits sturdy enough to hold up during cooking.

I'd like to dedicate this signature recipe to the Armenian origin of the quince, as well as to lamb, the traditional meat of the Armenian table. It's tangy yet sweet, buttery yet savory; you've never tasted anything like this before. Prepare ahead, if desired; these dolmas are delicious even when reheated.

4 large fresh quinces

1 teaspoon fresh lemon juice

½ yellow onion, finely chopped

2 tablespoons olive oil

¾ pound ground lamb

½ cup short-grain rice (Calrose rice)

¼ teaspoon ground allspice

½ teaspoon salt

¼ teaspoon ground black pepper

¼ cup water

One 14½-ounce can peeled, diced tomatoes

2 cloves garlic, minced

Juice of 2 lemons

2 teaspoons dried mint

Plain yogurt

1. Square off the irregularly shaped quinces by cutting off the tops and bottoms. Reserve the tops in water with 1 teaspoon lemon juice added. Place the quinces in a glass or ceramic microwave-safe dish with enough water to cover half of the fruit. Cover and microwave on high for 15 minutes, flipping once during cooking. Remove and let stand, uncovered, until the fruit is cool enough to handle. (If you don't have a microwave, bake the whole quinces according to the instructions on page 29 for 1 hour, and then core them.)

2. Using a sharp knife, melon baller, or peach pitter, hollow out the core of each softened whole quince. Be careful to preserve the fruit whole; remove even the slightest traces of rock-hard core while retaining as much pulp as possible. Set aside.

3. Sauté the onion in the olive oil in a skillet over medium heat until tender, about 8 minutes. Transfer to a large mixing bowl. Add the lamb, rice, allspice, salt, black pepper, and water. Mix well. I use my hands; it's quick and easy.

4. Stuff the quinces with the lamb mixture and place them in a large heavy-bottomed pot or a deep-sided pan large enough to hold them in one layer but small enough to pack them close together.

5. Combine the tomatoes, garlic, lemon juice, and mint in a mixing bowl. Pour this mixture over the stuffed quinces. If necessary, add more water to just cover the fruit with liquid. Squeeze the reserved quince tops anywhere in the pan. Place a dinner plate, bottom side up, over the stuffed quinces to secure them, cover the pot, and quickly bring to a boil. Lower the heat and simmer for 45 minutes, or until the quinces are cooked through and tender.

6. Remove the stuffed quinces to a serving platter or individual dishes and cap with the tops. Serve hot, garnished with a dollop of yogurt. A fresh tossed green salad dressed with extra-virgin olive oil and fresh lemon juice completes this satisfying meal.

Duck Breasts
with Quince-Sambal Chutney

serves 4

From east to west, cooks have prepared sauces from quince and served them on roasted fowl. In Britain, quince sauce is a traditional accompaniment to partridge, and the French roast whole quail with slices of the fruit. Moist, meaty duck breasts come alive with this stealthily hot fruit topping. If you have only one fresh quince, this is the recipe to try.

for the quince:
3 cups water

¼ cup sugar

1 tablespoon fresh lemon juice

One 3-inch cinnamon stick

½ star anise pod

1 medium or large fresh quince, peeled, cored, and cut into ½-inch-thick wedges

for the chutney:
1 tablespoon quince poaching liquid, reserved from quince preparation

½ to 1 teaspoon sambal oelek (see Note)

1 small clove garlic, minced

1 tablespoon finely chopped fresh mint, or 1 teaspoon dried

½ teaspoon grated peeled fresh ginger

½ teaspoon coarse salt

½ teaspoon white vinegar

Dash of ground cinnamon, optional

for the duck:

Four 6-ounce boneless whole duck breasts, thawed

Coarse salt and freshly ground black pepper

1 tablespoon thinly sliced green onion, white and light green parts only

1 tablespoon chopped fresh flat-leaf parsley

1. Prepare the quince a day or so ahead of time. Combine the water, sugar, lemon juice, cinnamon stick, star anise, and quince in a heavy-bottomed pot. Quickly bring to a boil, then lower the heat and simmer uncovered for 1 hour. Discard the cinnamon stick and star anise pod and cool to room temperature. Cover and refrigerate the quince in its syrup until you are ready to prepare the duck.

2. Preheat the oven to 400°F.

3. To prepare the chutney, drain the quince, reserving the poaching liquid. Transfer the fruit to a pretty serving bowl. Add 1 tablespoon poaching liquid, ½ teaspoon sambal oelek, and the garlic, mint, ginger, salt, and vinegar. Toss to mix. Taste and add the remaining ½ teaspoon sambal oelek and a dash of cinnamon, if desired. Set aside.

4. Season the duck breasts with salt and black pepper. Heat a skillet over medium-high heat. Place the duck breasts, skin side down, in the pan and sear for 2 minutes or until the skin is golden brown. Cook the opposite side for 1 minute.

5. Transfer the breasts to a foil-lined baking pan, skin side up, insert a meat thermometer, and bake in the middle of the oven for 15 minutes, or until the thermometer registers a temperature of 160°F. Place the breasts on a work surface, skin side down. Cut the duck diagonally across the grain into thin slices.

6. Divide the duck evenly among four plates; top with the quince-sambal chutney and garnish with green onion and parsley. Serve immediately with a simple salad and grain of your choosing.

Note: Sambal oelek can be found in most supermarkets nationwide in the international foods section. It is a fresh Chinese chili sauce much like salsa, but hotter—much hotter! If you can't find it, you can substitute fresh chili paste.

Halibut and Quince-Stuffed Phyllo with Lemon Beurre Blanc

serves 6

White fish and poached quince are a successful couple, playing off each other's looks and flavors. The North Atlantic haddock is my favorite white fish; unfortunately it's virtually unknown west of the Mississippi. Halibut, red snapper, and tilapia all bake, moist and flaky, in the golden phyllo pockets.

Chopped steamed broccoli or a bitter green vegetable makes an excellent accompaniment.

for the quince:
1 pound fresh quince, poached according to the directions on page 27
(2 cups poached quince, drained and diced)

for the filling:
1¼ pounds halibut, bones removed, divided into 6 equal pieces
Coarse salt and freshly ground white pepper
⅓ cup finely chopped yellow onion
2 teaspoons olive oil
1 small jalapeño pepper, stem and seeds removed, finely chopped
2 tablespoons finely chopped fresh flat-leaf parsley
1½ tablespoons butter, cut into 6 pieces

for the shell:
1 package phyllo dough (20 sheets)
⅜ pound (1½ sticks) butter, melted

for the sauce:

2 shallots, minced

½ cup dry white wine, Champagne, or dry vermouth

¼ cup fresh lemon juice (2 lemons)

¼ pound (1 stick) unsalted butter, cubed

½ teaspoon coarse salt

Freshly ground white pepper

1 tablespoon snipped fresh dill

1. Prepare the quince as directed.
2. Preheat the oven to 350°F. Wash the fish, blot dry with paper towels, and season with salt and white pepper to taste. Set aside.
3. Sauté the onion in the olive oil in a small skillet until golden brown, about 5 minutes. Transfer to a medium-sized mixing bowl. Add the quince, jalapeño, and parsley. Toss to combine and set aside.
4. Unwrap the phyllo dough and place it near the flat work surface where you will assemble the phyllo packages. Cover immediately with a double layer of plastic wrap and a clean, dampened kitchen towel to prevent the dough from drying out.
5. Arrange the dough, seasoned fish, quince mixture, 6 butter pieces, and melted butter around your work area, and set out baking sheets and a pastry brush. Organizing yourself in this way will facilitate the speed and assembly of the phyllo pockets.
6. To assemble, lay 1 phyllo sheet on the flat work surface, with the short side closest to you and the long side extending away from you. Using a pastry brush and working quickly, brush the sheet with melted butter. Place a second sheet on top and brush it with butter; repeat until you have layered 3 sheets of dough.
7. Place a piece of fish in the center of the phyllo sheet, approximately ¼ of the way from the short end of the dough edge nearest you, keeping about 1-inch margins on each side. Top the fish with one-sixth of the quince mixture. Top with a cube of butter. Fold the bottom edge of the dough over the filling. As neatly as possible, fold each of the long sides in and roll the phyllo up and away from you like a jelly roll. Brush the exterior with melted butter and set the stuffed phyllo pocket, seam side down, on a baking sheet. Repeat until all six phyllo pockets are assembled.

8. Bake in the middle of the oven for 25 minutes, or until golden.
9. While the phyllo pockets are baking, prepare the sauce. Combine the shallots and spirit in a small nonreactive saucepan. Heat to a simmer and cook until the liquid is reduced by half. Add the lemon juice; reduce again by half, or until syrupy. Strain through a fine sieve. Return to the warm pan. Slowly whisk in the butter, a few cubes at a time, until all of the butter is well combined. Stir in the salt and white pepper to taste. If you need to reheat, do so over very low heat.
10. Set each baked phyllo pocket on an individual serving plate. Spoon an equal portion of sauce on top of each. Garnish with fresh dill and serve immediately.

Lamb Rib Chops
with Minted Quince Pan Sauce

serves 4

You don't need a special occasion to enjoy lamb rib chops. Paired with the classic duo of quince and mint, this midweek meal comes together quickly. Serve with a baked yam and side of steamed green beans or broccolini (broccolini is baby broccoli and my current favorite) tossed in butter and seasoned with salt and pepper. So easy, delicious, and elegant; your family may wonder what the special occasion is all about!

for the quince:
½ pound fresh quince, poached according to the directions on page 27
(1 cup poached quince, drained and coarsely chopped)

for the lamb:
Eight 1-inch-thick lamb rib chops
Coarse salt and freshly ground black pepper
1 tablespoon butter
1 tablespoon olive oil
1 red onion, halved and sliced thin (about 2 cups)
½ cup chicken broth
½ teaspoon dried mint
¼ cup finely chopped fresh mint

1. Prepare the quince as directed.
2. Preheat the oven to 250°F.
3. Season the lamb chops with salt and black pepper. Melt the butter with the olive oil in a large skillet over medium-high heat. Add the lamb chops and cook to

desired doneness, about 2 minutes per side for medium rare. Transfer the chops to a baking dish and keep warm in the oven while preparing the sauce (do not clean the skillet).

4. Sauté the onion in the skillet for a few minutes, scraping up any browned bits; then add the quince, broth, and dried mint. Simmer over medium heat until the liquid is slightly reduced and the onion is tender, about 5 minutes. Add half of the fresh mint and cook for 1 minute. Adjust the seasonings to taste.

5. Place two lamb chops on each of four plates. Spoon enough sauce on top to cover, garnish with the remaining fresh mint, and serve immediately.

Savory Condiments

Quince and Red Pepper Chutney

makes 4 cups

Sweet-spicy cooked fruit condiments originated in India. Britons who were introduced to them during the colonial period brought the flavors home to British tables as a surefire way to zip up an otherwise bland meal.

Tailor-made for chutney, quince is a good vehicle for spice because of its texture and mild flavor.

In 1995, I stumbled across this recipe in the October issue of *Country Living*, and it became a family favorite on the first try. Although it's a delicious accompaniment to grilled or baked meat or fowl, this festive fall chutney is out of this world served with pâtés, on burgers, on turkey sandwiches, or to liven up cheese-and-bread combos. Best of all, it can be made ahead. Just seal and keep refrigerated until serving. It freezes well, too.

1 tablespoon olive oil

1 yellow onion, diced (about 1 cup)

1 large red bell pepper, diced (about 1 cup)

1¾ to 2 pounds fresh quince, peeled, cored, and diced (about 6 cups)

½ cup raisins

¼ cup firmly packed light brown sugar

¼ cup apple cider vinegar

1 cup water

1 teaspoon yellow mustard seeds

½ teaspoon ground coriander

½ teaspoon crushed red pepper flakes

1 teaspoon coarse salt

¼ teaspoon ground black pepper

One 1 × 3-inch strip lemon rind

1. In a large heavy-bottomed pot, heat the olive oil over medium heat. Add the onion and red pepper and sauté for 5 minutes, or until softened. Stir in the quince, raisins, brown sugar, cider vinegar, water, mustard seeds, coriander, red pepper flakes, salt, black pepper, and lemon rind.

2. Bring to a boil, then lower the heat to medium-low and cook, stirring occasionally, until the quince pieces soften, 20 minutes. It may seem like there is too little liquid, but the fruit will express juices as it cooks down. Simmer until the quince is tender and the liquid is reduced to a syrup that just moistens the fruit, about 40 minutes. Discard the lemon rind.

3. Serve at room temperature. If making ahead, transfer to an airtight container and refrigerate or freeze.

Fresh Ginger and Quince Pomegranate Chutney

makes 2½ cups

Images of pomegranates adorn entries and archways of Armenian churches throughout Eastern Anatolia and the Caucasus. But pomegranates share similarities with quinces beyond being ancient neighbors. Both fruits ripen in autumn and boast extremely high beneficial antioxidant content. As with many of the flavor combinations suggested in this collection, quince and pomegranate have been longtime bedfellows.

Pomegranate vinegar lends a strong flavor to this chutney and offers the perfect backdrop against which to showcase glistening quince pieces, peppery fresh ginger, and sweet currants.

The vinegar fumes can be unpleasantly strong while cooking, so make sure your kitchen is properly ventilated.

¼ cup peeled fresh ginger, cut into fine ¾-inch-long matchsticks
1½ pounds fresh quince, peels left on, cored, and cut into ¼-inch dice (about 3 cups)
1 cup pomegranate vinegar (see Note)
1 cup sugar
½ cup currants

1. Place the ginger in a large heavy-bottomed pot with 4 cups water. Bring to a boil, uncovered. Boil vigorously for 1 minute, then drain.
2. Return the ginger to the pot. Add the quince, vinegar, sugar, and currants. Bring to a boil, stirring to dissolve the sugar, and then lower the heat and simmer uncovered, stirring occasionally, until the quince is tender and the liquid is reduced to a syrup that just moistens the fruit, 35 to 40 minutes. Make sure to provide proper ventilation.

3. Remove from the heat and let stand until ready to serve. If preparing ahead, store in an airtight container and chill. The chutney will keep up to 2 weeks in the refrigerator without changing flavor. It also freezes well.

Note: Pomegranate vinegar is sold in Middle Eastern markets and can often be found at your local supermarket in the international foods section. Or make your own by combining 1 cup fresh pomegranate seeds and 2 cups white wine vinegar in a clean, sterilized quart jar with a lid. Crush the seeds slightly by stirring. Place the jar on a windowsill and steep for 8 to 10 days. Strain through dampened cheesecloth. Transfer to clean, sterilized glass bottles or jars, seal tightly, and store in a cool dark place or refrigerate.

Quick Quince Chutney

makes ¾ cup

Festive red, sweet quince preserve gets sassy with a few quick and easy additions. I particularly like this flavor boost spooned over grilled or roasted chicken and turkey.

½ cup Quince Jam (page 124), or store-bought
2 tablespoons grated white onion
½ teaspoon grated peeled fresh ginger
Pinch of coarse salt
Smidgen of Aleppo pepper or cayenne

Combine the ingredients in a serving bowl and blend until mixed. Spoon over turkey or chicken breast or add to a turkey or chicken sandwich.

Tangy-Sweet Quince Relish

makes 3 pints

Revel in this deep ruby-red relish. Medieval cooks valued quince relish as an accompaniment to roasted meats. It's divine with cheese, pork, or ham. But don't stop there—try it on hamburgers, hot dogs, and poultry. Top a baked sweet potato or spread it on a bagel with cream cheese for breakfast. Go ahead; eat it straight out of the jar!

2 pounds fresh quince, peels left on, cored, and grated (about 7 cups)

1¼ cups white wine vinegar

1 cup red wine vinegar

3½ cups sugar

1 tablespoon chopped peeled fresh ginger

½ teaspoon ground cloves

¼ teaspoon ground nutmeg

1 teaspoon salt

1 teaspoon ground black pepper

¼ teaspoon cayenne

1. Combine the quince, vinegars, sugar, ginger, cloves, nutmeg, salt, black pepper, and cayenne in a large heavy-bottomed pot. Bring to a boil, stirring to dissolve the sugar. Lower the heat and simmer uncovered, stirring frequently, until just enough liquid remains to cover the relish when jarred, 1 to 1¼ hours. Make sure to provide proper ventilation; the vinegar fumes can be unpleasantly strong.
2. Ladle through a wide-mouthed funnel into sterilized half-pint jars. Process (see page 114), or simply cover with lids and screw tops and keep refrigerated. Once opened and chilled, the relish will keep for several months. This relish makes a great holiday gift for the connoisseurs on your list.

Spreads and Preserves

Raw quince will *oxidize*, or brown, quickly. However, as soon as the fruit begins to cook, the brown disappears. Many recipes suggest that you cover the cut fruit with lemon water in order to stop this process. As long as I'm not planning to take a break between cutting and cooking the fruit, I omit this step because it has no effect on the taste or the outcome of the dish.

Fiery Quince-Tomato Spread

makes 3 pints

Combining quince and tomato may seem odd, so I studied the original recipe for months before I gave it a try. Boy, am I glad I did! Initially the more-savory-than-sweet spread was good, but once I added pepper, it caught fire. A serving on hearty-grain toast, rye, or pumpernickel with a soft, delicate cheese—mascarpone is my favorite—will transport you across the pond. It's the consummate continental breakfast. Garnish with fresh basil, if desired.

2 pounds fresh quince, peeled, cored, and grated (about 7 cups)

Two 14½-ounce cans peeled, diced tomatoes, mashed (about 3½ cups pulp and juice), or

2 pounds fresh tomatoes (6 large), blanched, skins and seeds removed, and mashed

1 cup sugar

¼ cup fresh lemon juice (2 lemons)

1½ teaspoons salt

¾ teaspoon crushed red pepper flakes

¼ teaspoon freshly ground black pepper

1. Combine the shredded quince, mashed tomatoes, sugar, lemon juice, salt, and red pepper flakes in a large heavy-bottomed pot. Bring to a boil over medium-high heat, then turn the heat down and simmer, uncovered and stirring often, for about 1 hour. Add the black pepper and taste. Adjust sugar and salt, if desired.
2. Ladle through a wide-mouthed funnel into sterilized half-pint jars. Process (see page 114), or simply cover with lids and screw tops and keep refrigerated. Chilled, this versatile spread keeps for 1 month, although I doubt it will be around that long!

How to Process Preserves

Ancient kitchen wisdom and modern techniques come together to help you preserve homemade goodies safely, easily, and, importantly, without additives. Unlike my grandmother, who single-handedly tackled bushels of quinces, I use recipes that call for no more than 2 pounds of fresh fruit. At this juncture in the quince's renaissance, fresh quinces may not be readily available in much of the country. And when they are available, the cost per fruit can be pricy. Plus, preserving smaller quantities of fruit helps prevent fatigue and potential mistakes—the process takes about 4 hours and can be stretched into a multiday process without worry of failure.

Following the rules of safe canning is important, and having the right equipment on hand will make the process easier (see KITCHEN TOOLS). Always follow the manufacturer's directions.

To sterilize the jars, submerge clean jars in boiling water or set them on a baking tray in a 250°F oven, with tops open, for at least 10 minutes, or until ready to fill. (I use the oven method because my city tap water leaves a white mineral residue on the jars when they are boiled in it.) Heat the lids in hot, but not boiling, water (about 180°F), and keep them submerged until placed on the filled jars.

Fill a water-bath canner with hot tap water, lower the jar rack, cover, and begin heating to a boil. It's best to have the water bath simmering so you can process the hot sealed jars immediately. When the preserves are ready, use a wide-mouth funnel to fill the jars with hot preserves to within ¼ to ½ inch from the top. Wipe the jar rims with a clean damp cloth to remove any preserves. Cover with a new rubber-rimmed canning lid and close securely but not too tightly.

Using a jar lifter, submerge the filled jars in the canner. The rack will keep them from touching each other. If necessary, add more water, so that 2 inches of water covers the top of the jars when submerged. Start counting your water-bath processing time when the water reaches a full rolling boil. Cover the canner and process for 20 minutes if at sea level (refer to the manufacturer's directions for higher elevations). Use the jar lifter to remove the jars and set them on a towel to cool. As the jars cool, the lids will pop or "ping," indicating a good seal. Label with the date and store in a cool, dry place. To be safe, use all preserves within 1 year of the date of processing.

Simply Quince

Autumn-Spiced Quince Butter

makes about 2 cups

Smooth, thick fruit butters offer a silky, full-flavored spread that's less sweet than traditional jams or jellies.

Apple butter is the flagship of all butters, but once you've tried my rich mahogany-red Quince Butter, I bet you'll never go back. Made from the Quince-Apple Sauce recipe (page 63), this spread is not tart yet not noticeably sweet, either. It's spiced with a medley of nutmeg, allspice, cloves, and cinnamon that will add tasty variety to your table.

4 cups Quince-Apple Sauce (page 63), warmed and puréed until smooth
¼ cup apple cider or unsweetened juice
½ cup firmly packed light brown sugar
¼ cup sugar plus ¼ cup, depending on taste
¼ teaspoon ground cinnamon
Pinch of ground nutmeg
Smidgen of ground allspice
Sprinkle of ground cloves

1. Preheat the oven to 300°F.
2. Combine the warm Quince-Apple Sauce (the sauce will purée smoother and easier if it is warm), cider or juice, brown sugar, ¼ cup of the sugar, and the cinnamon, nutmeg, allspice, and cloves in a mixing bowl. Push the pulp through a fine sieve to remove any remaining lumps of fruit, if desired. If you don't mind a few fruit chunks in your spread, omit this process. Pour the mixture into an 8-inch square baking pan.
3. Bake for 2½ hours, stirring occasionally, until the quince butter is brick red throughout and has the consistency you prefer. Taste; add additional sugar 1 tablespoon at a time, if desired.

4. Ladle through a wide-mouthed funnel into sterilized half-pint jars. Process (see page 114), or simply cover with lids and screw tops and keep refrigerated. Chilled, the quince butter will keep for up to 2 months.

Quince Fruit Leather

makes two 11 × 17-inch sheets

Generations of Armenian children have grown up eating dried fruit leather called *bastegh*. Most of us have memories of our grandmother spreading mysterious Concord grape juice slurry on clean bedsheets, laying them on the parlor floor for a day, and then hanging the purple-coated sheets on the clothesline to dry in the sun. But when I tried drying quince bastegh the "old way," it came out tasting like laundry detergent!

Traditionally, bastegh is eaten rolled around walnuts as an afternoon snack, or you can add it to your children's lunch boxes for a special treat.

Make this fruit leather from scratch using fresh quinces, water, and sugar (Method 1), or with quince poaching liquid reserved from another cooking session (Method 2).

METHOD 1 (STEPS 1–11)

> 1¾ to 2 pounds fresh quince
>
> 12 cups water
>
> 1 cup sugar

METHOD 2 (STEPS 6–11)

> Quince poaching liquid (page 27), reserved from another recipe

TO THICKEN (BOTH METHODS):

> ¾ cup white all-purpose flour
>
> Cornstarch

1. If using Method 1, peel, core, and quarter the quinces. Reserve the cores and peels in a large heavy-bottomed pot. Add cold water to cover, about 4 cups; set aside.

2. Dice or grate the quince quarters and combine them with the remaining 8 cups water and the sugar in a second large heavy-bottomed pot. Line two 11 × 17-inch rimmed baking trays with parchment paper and set aside.

3. Bring the peels and cores to a boil. Lower the heat to a gentle simmer and cook for 40 minutes. Strain through a sieve double lined with dampened cheesecloth and set over a bowl to collect the juice. Discard the fruit trimmings and cool the juice (about 2 cups) to room temperature.

4. Bring the quince-sugar mixture to a boil over medium heat, stirring to dissolve the sugar. Lower the heat and gently simmer for 1½ hours, or until the fruit is very tender. Cool for about 10 minutes, then transfer to the bowl of a food processor and purée until smooth (about 4 cups purée).

5. Preheat the oven to 150°F.

6. If using Method 1, measure the quince purée and reserved juice separately and add the amounts. If using Method 2, measure (in cups) the quantity of poaching liquid. This recipe assumes 6 cups quince liquid to ¾ cup flour. Adjust the quantity of flour to how many cups quince liquid you have (for example, 4 cups poaching liquid to ½ cup flour).

7. Place the quince purée and reserved juice (if using Method 1) OR poaching liquid (if using Method 2) in a mixing bowl. (The procedure for both methods is the same from this point forward.) Chill the mixture slightly, or the flour will clump. Slowly whisk in the flour, ¼ cup at a time, until all of the flour is added and well blended. The mixture will turn whitish in color.

8. Pour the whitish quince-flour mixture into a clean, heavy-bottomed pot. Whisking constantly, bring to a rolling boil and boil for about 1 minute. The mixture will thicken like pudding. Ladle half of the mixture onto each prepared baking tray and spread evenly, about ⅛ to ¼ inch thick.

9. Dry, one tray at a time, in the middle of the oven for 6 or 7 hours. The fruit leather will be dry, but pliable.

10. Remove from the oven; peel away the parchment paper and continue to air-dry, if necessary, on a wire rack. (Now is the time for the "old ways"; go ahead and hang it on the line.)

11. Dust lightly with cornstarch. Cut into strips, roll, or fold as desired. Store sealed in a plastic bag or airtight container.

Potpourri of Quince Marmalades: Lemon, Orange, and Ginger

makes 2 pints

Marmalades originated in Portugal, where early cooks added citrus peels to a quince base. Those cooks knew that the mild taste and high pectin content of quince offered the perfect canvas for small additions of stronger flavors. Preparing small batches of marmalade doesn't take much time and yields enough for friends and family.

BASIC QUINCE MARMALADE

3 cups water

2 cups sugar

1½ to 1¾ pounds fresh quince, peeled, cored, and grated (5 to 6 cups)

QUINCE-LEMON MARMALADE

A hint of vanilla mellows the zippy tang of lemon. For a gentler-tasting spread, use a Meyer lemon.

Ingredients for Basic Quince Marmalade, plus:

1 small fresh lemon, or ½ large fresh lemon, or 1 fresh Meyer lemon,

washed, seeded, and finely chopped in a food processor (about ½ cup)

One 1-inch piece vanilla bean, split lengthwise with seeds scraped into the mixture, or

1 teaspoon vanilla extract

Quince-Orange Marmalade

Golden quince dances with flecks of orange and flavor in this version, which is my personal favorite. It's sweeter than traditional orange marmalade, but still strong enough to unclog the drowsy morning palate.

Ingredients for Basic Quince Marmalade (reduce water to 1½ cups), plus:
½ cup orange juice
½ fresh orange, washed, seeded, and grated (about ¾ cup)

Quince-Ginger Marmalade

Striking a perfect balance between golden fruit and pungent root, this is for the ginger lovers in your life.

Ingredients for Basic Quince Marmalade, plus:
3 tablespoons fresh lemon juice (1 to 2 lemons)
1½ tablespoons grated or finely chopped peeled fresh ginger
½ teaspoon coarse salt

1. Combine the ingredients for the marmalade of your choice in a large heavy-bottomed pot. Bring to a boil, stirring to dissolve the sugar; lower the heat and simmer for 1 hour, or until most of the liquid is reduced. These marmalades are chunky, but should not be cooked dry, so be sure a sufficient quantity of liquid remains to cover the fruit.
2. Ladle through a wide-mouthed funnel into sterilized half-pint jars. Process (see page 114), or simply cover with lids and screw tops and keep refrigerated. Chilled, the marmalade will keep for up to 2 months.

Conserves of Quince in Wine and Brandy

makes 1½ to 2 pints

Conserves are elegant jams with sophisticated additions such as ginger, brandy, rum, and almost always nuts. I adapted this chunky, radiant conserve from a recipe published in 1982 by Jocasta Innes in *Your Country Kitchen*. Enjoy it spread on toast or cascade it over a log of tangy goat cheese and set at the center of your holiday table.

2 fresh lemons, juiced (¼ cup), then peeled (reserving the rinds), fruit discarded

1½ cups dry white wine

1½ cups boiling water

2¼ cups sugar

1½ to 1¾ pounds fresh quince, peeled, cored, and diced (about 3½ cups)

1 pound fresh hard apples (do not use McIntosh or cooking apples), peeled, cored, and diced (2 to 2½ cups)

2 teaspoons brandy

1. Combine the lemon rinds, wine, and boiling water in a bowl; steep for 30 minutes.
2. Transfer the lemon-wine mixture into a large heavy-bottomed pot. Stir in the lemon juice and sugar. Bring to a boil and boil hard for about 10 minutes, until slightly syrupy. Use a slotted spoon to remove the lemon peels and discard.
3. Add the quince. Simmer, stirring occasionally, for 30 minutes; then add the apples. Continue to simmer, stirring frequently, for 40 minutes, or until the fruit is tender and the syrup thick. Stir in the brandy.
4. Ladle through a wide-mouthed funnel into sterilized half-pint jars. Process (see page 114), or simply cover with lids and screw tops and keep refrigerated. Chilled, the conserves will keep for up to 2 months.

Quince-Cranberry-Walnut Conserves

makes about 3 pints

This recipe was generously shared by Joyce Kierejczyk of Fresno, California. Joyce is a home preserver extraordinaire. She puts up more than a thousand jars of jam and jelly every year—just for the fun of it! Many of her fruit preserves are reduced-sugar mixes. This conserve contains very little sugar. It's almost tart! So if you are looking for something new and unique to grace your table for the Thanksgiving celebration, it is just the ticket. Or, roll it into pork filets like a roulade—your family will love it.

3 cups water
1½ cups sugar plus ¼ cup, depending on taste
¼ cup fresh lemon juice (2 lemons)
1¾ to 2 pounds fresh quince, peeled, cored, and grated (about 7 cups)
2 cups fresh cranberries
1 cup coarsely chopped walnuts, sifted to remove nut dust

1. Combine the water, sugar, and lemon juice in a large heavy-bottomed pot. Bring to a boil, stirring to dissolve the sugar. Add the quince and simmer uncovered for 1 hour. Stir in the cranberries and continue to simmer for about 30 minutes. Add the walnuts 5 minutes before finishing. Taste for sweetness; add 1 tablespoon sugar at a time up to an additional ¼ cup, if desired.
2. Ladle through a wide-mouthed funnel into sterilized half-pint jars. Process (see page 114), or simply cover with lids and screw tops and keep refrigerated. Chilled, the conserves will keep for up to 2 months.

Jam Session

I love making preserves. Crisp autumn breezes propel me into the kitchen, as they did my grandmother and her mother before her. The continuity of the tradition is as priceless as the homemade goodies my family and friends will enjoy during the subsequent months. There's nothing quite like rolling up your sleeves and getting into the kitchen for a day of preserving sun-ripened quince.

The qualities that make raw quince difficult to process—hardness, tartness, and astringency—are what make it perfect for making jam. Loaded with natural pectin, quince preserves the old-fashioned way: 100 percent natural, without artificial additives.

Of course, if you live in California or near a Middle Eastern grocer, you may think, why bother putting up your own quince preserves when you can purchase tasty import varieties at the store?

A slow and sensuous, strange and beautiful alchemy occurs when preserving quince—a magic that doesn't occur with any other fruit. Slow-cooked with sugar, quince initially looks and smells like applesauce, then like caramel candy. The process culminates in rich, ruby-red preserves, distinct in taste and texture from anything else on earth. You just can't buy the one-of-a-kind flavors and aromas of quince. But you *can* quince with me and begin a tradition that you will look forward to every year.

Quince Jam

During my first autumn living on the central coast of California, a new friend, originally from Serbia, told me she loved quince and that her mother made quince preserves every fall. As soon as fresh quinces appeared in the market, she taught me her family recipe. Since that day of quincing, Serbian-style, this recipe became a staple in my kitchen. Friends and relatives receive a jar every holiday season and reward me with enthusiastic thanks. It's easy, sweet but not too sweet, and the jam sparkles with red-orange glow and rich quince flavor.

5 cups water

3½ cups sugar

2 pounds fresh quince, peeled, cored, and grated (about 7 cups)

¼ cup fresh lemon juice (2 lemons)

1. Combine the water and sugar in a large heavy-bottomed pot. Bring to a boil, stirring to dissolve the sugar, then simmer vigorously for 10 minutes to thicken the syrup slightly.
2. Add the quince and lemon juice. Simmer gently, stirring often, for about 1 hour, or to the jell point (see page 125).
3. Ladle through a wide-mouthed funnel into sterilized half-pint jars. Process (see page 114), or simply cover with lids and screw tops and keep refrigerated. Chilled, this jam will keep for months.

Finding the Jell Point

The jell point is the moment in the cooking process when the preserve will be soft enough to jiggle; not too firm and not too syrupy. Cooking a fruit mixture for a significant time with lots of sugar and a little lemon juice reduces the moisture content through evaporation and brings the pectin strands, released by the quinces during cooking, close enough together to bind again into a jell. Sounds simple, but reaching the jell point can be a bit tricky. The major ingredient not listed in the preserve recipes is patience!

There are three ways to test your fruit preserve for readiness to jell: with a candy thermometer, a cold plate, or a cold spoon.

The candy thermometer test: This method is the most accurate. Technically, the jell point is 8° above the boiling point (212°F). At sea level, the jell point is 220°F; at altitudes higher than 1,000 feet, add 8° to the temperature at which water boils. Use a thermometer with a protective base and a clip to hold it firmly in place.

The cold plate test: Drop about a teaspoon of fruit mixture on an ice-cold plate. If it retains its shape and stays together when pushed gently with your finger, it's done.

The cold spoon test: Dip an ice-cold metal spoon into your hot fruit mix and allow the mixture to run off the spoon. When it slides off the spoon in one sheet, the fruit is done.

Ottoman Quince Preserve

makes 2 to 2 ½ pints

This is my Grandma Mooradian's quince preserve recipe. In 1907, at age nine, Grandma made the arduous land and sea journey to the United States from a small farming village in the Ottoman Empire.

Her destination was Whitinsville, Massachusetts, a small mill town in the Blackstone Valley, where her father had settled several years earlier and built an authentic Turkish bathhouse. The women of the family arrived with little more than their clothes, but they did bring optimism, a strong work ethic, and a deep knowledge of farming and food preparation.

At the beginning of the twentieth century, many homes across America had quince trees growing in their yards, and soon my family owned a home that boasted a fruit-bearing quince, too. My great-grandmother and her daughter knew just what to do with the sun-ripened fruit because it grew in the Anatolian village they had left behind. (Today, Turkey is the largest commercial grower of quince in the world.)

The tradition of putting up quince preserves and jellies rooted anew in Massachusetts. It's a family tradition many of us share, no matter what distant shore we claim as origin. A Turkish associate said, "These are exactly how my mother used to make them." For a taste trip to an Istanbul café, this is the choice. The preserves are a deep, almost garnet color, and the thin slices of fruit are mouthwatering.

2 pounds fresh quince (see Note)
8 cups water
¼ cup fresh lemon juice (2 lemons)
Sugar

1. Peel, core, and quarter the quinces. Place the cores and peels in a large heavy-bottomed pot with 8 cups water. Bring to a boil, then lower the heat and simmer gently for 40 minutes.

2. Meanwhile, cut the quince quarters into thin slices, approximately ¼ inch thick and ½ inch long, and immediately put the slices in cold water with 2 tablespoons of the lemon juice added to reduce discoloring. Set aside.

3. Strain the cores-peels mixture through a sieve double-lined with moistened cheesecloth and set over a bowl. Press out all of the juice; return the juice to the large heavy-bottomed pot.

4. Drain the reserved quince slices and transfer them to the pot with the juice. Heat to a simmer and cook gently, uncovered, until the fruit pieces are tender, about 30 minutes.

5. Using a metal measuring tool (plastic may crack), measure (in cups) the quantity of quince juice and slices. After measuring, return to the original pot and add ¾ cup sugar for every 1 cup of cooked fruit and juice.

6. Over medium heat, stir until the sugar is dissolved and then simmer, uncovered, stirring often to keep from scorching, for 1 hour. Add the remaining 2 tablespoons lemon juice and begin to test for jelling (see page 125).

7. Ladle through a wide-mouthed funnel into sterilized half-pint jars. Process (see page 114), or simply cover with lids and screw tops and keep refrigerated. Chilled, this preserve will keep for months.

Note: If the raw fruit is really tough to slice, you can use the slicing blade of a food processor. However, this generally results in slices too large and thick to be appetizing. If so, hand-cut into smaller slices before cooking.

Quince Jellies: Classic Quince-Apple, Spiced Quince, and Subtle Quince-Rose

makes 2 to 3 pints

Jelly is a sweet, transparent mixture made from fruit juice and sugar. Quince jelly delights the eye with its crystalline ruby color, and the appetite with its moist, quivering tenderness. A jar makes a well-appreciated homemade gift.

Jelly is an excellent choice if you have "backyard fruit"—fruit that is badly blemished, or has been invaded by pests. I know all about that; my family didn't use pesticides. For jelly, you don't peel or core the quince, so you can cut around imperfections without compromising the recipe.

Making large quantities of jelly is traditional, because home preservers, like my grandmother, had a quince tree in their yard and an overabundance of fruit. But large yields can be daunting, so I recommend starting with a smaller batch. Multiply any of these three versions if you have the fruit and are willing to devote a couple of days to the process. Being able to grace your breakfast table for the coming year with delicious quince spread will make all the effort worthwhile.

BASIC QUINCE JELLY

2 pounds fresh quince, stems and blemishes removed, coarsely chopped,
including peels and cores (8 to 9 cups)
8 cups water
2 tablespoons fresh lemon juice (1 lemon)
Sugar

Classic Quince-Apple Jelly

My grandmother always added a few apples to her quince jelly. The flavors complement each other well and result in delicious jelly.

Ingredients for Basic Quince Jelly, plus:
2 firm red apples (do not use McIntosh apples)

Spiced Quince Jelly

If you love a strong quince flavor, this is the jelly for you!

Ingredients for Basic Quince Jelly, plus:
One 3-inch cinnamon stick
One 1-inch chunk peeled fresh ginger
4 whole cloves

Subtle Quince-Rose Jelly

Whenever I meet someone who loves quince, we inevitably end up sharing our quince memories. Often, folks with British roots fondly remember their mothers or grandmothers making quince-rose jelly. My version of this old-fashioned jelly has just a hint of rose flavor, one that's alluring rather than overpowering. A friend commented that it is much better than her mother's. Now that's success!

Ingredients for Basic Quince Jelly, plus:
¼ cup dried rose petals (see Note)

1. Put the chopped quince, including peels, seeds, and cores (these sections are very high in natural pectin), into a large heavy-bottomed pot with enough cold water to cover, about 8 cups. Stir in 1 tablespoon of the lemon juice.
2. For quince-apple jelly, cut the apples the same way and add them to the pot. For spiced quince jelly, add the cinnamon stick, ginger, and cloves. For quince-rose

jelly, stir in the rose petals. In every case, add additional cold water to cover, if necessary.

3. Bring to a boil, then lower the heat and gently simmer, stirring often from the bottom so the fruit does not burn, for 40 minutes. This first-cook stage releases the juices and pectin from the fruit. It should be as brief and gentle as possible to avoid damaging the pectin strands. Remember, quince is high in natural pectin, and you won't be adding any artificial pectin to your jelly.

4. Line a large strainer with two layers of dampened cheesecloth and set it over a large bowl. Strain the fruit immediately. Allow the mash to drain for 1 to 2 hours. Don't squeeze or push the liquid out of the mash! The jelly will be cloudy if you do. (Most recipes ask you to drain many hours, sometimes even overnight, but the extra time does not make enough difference in yield to warrant the time. If you are working with a larger batch, consider using multiple strainers and collection bowls.) Often, I cover the collected juice tightly with plastic wrap and refrigerate it until I'm ready to make jelly. Chilled, the fruit juice will keep up to 3 days.

5. When you are ready to make the jelly, measure (in cups) the quantity of juice as you transfer it to a large heavy-bottomed pot. Add 1 cup sugar for every cup of juice (for example, 4 cups sugar to 4 cups juice). Sugar and natural fruit pectins are the jelling agents, so if you must lower the sugar content, don't dip below a ratio of ¾ cup sugar to 1 cup juice.

6. Heat to a simmer, stirring until the sugar is dissolved. Simmer uncovered, stirring frequently, for about 2 hours, or until the jell point. Skim any scum that forms at the top, especially toward the end of cooking. Depending on the size of your batch, this second-cook step can take a long time. The time it takes to reach the jell point may vary, often extending 1 hour or more when making larger quantities. As the jelly cooks it will change color from pink to ruby, and may even darken almost to garnet just before it's ready to jar. Add the remaining 1 tablespoon lemon juice within 15 minutes of reaching the jell point (see page 125).

7. Ladle through a wide-mouthed funnel into sterilized half-pint jars. Process (see page 114), or simply cover with lids and screw tops and keep refrigerated. Chilled, these jellies will keep for months.

Note: Dried rose petals can be purchased in most Middle Eastern groceries.

Compotes, Buckles,
Crisps, and Crumbles

Quince and Spiced Asian Pear Compote with Pomegranate, Yogurt, and Mint

serves 8

Fresh quince for dessert? Finding an edible raw quince ranks as a high priority for David Karp, the Fruit Detective, who lays claim to Karp's Sweet Quince, a South American variety he helped identify. Karp insists that the fruit from this tree is sweet and succulent enough to be eaten out of hand. Seedlings are being propagated and the variety can be purchased (see Sources). I've yet to taste one of the fruits, so I can't attest to the claim, although I hold Karp and his fruit expertise in high esteem. Certainly, Karp's variety is not readily available in markets; until it is, this simple, elegant compote is as close to eating sweet raw quince as I have found.

for the quince:

1 pound fresh quince, poached according to the directions on page 27
(about 2 cups poached quince, plus 1 cup poaching liquid)

for the compote:

1 large Asian pear, peeled, cored, and cut into ½-inch-thick wedges
1 cup water
3 whole cloves
½ cup fresh pomegranate seeds
1 cup Yogurt Cheese (recipe follows)
Sprigs of fresh mint

1. Prepare the quince as directed.
2. Combine the pear wedges, water, and cloves in a medium-sized saucepan. Bring to a boil, lower the heat, cover, and simmer for 15 to 20 minutes, or until the pear is

slightly translucent. Remove from the heat, drain through a sieve, discard the cloves, and set aside to cool.

3. Cut the cooled quince and pear wedges into ¼-inch-thick slices. Combine the fruit slices with the reserved poaching liquid in a bowl. Stir in the pomegranate seeds. Cover with plastic wrap and chill at least 1 hour before serving.

4. Spoon the chilled compote into individual serving dishes. Top with a dollop of Yogurt Cheese or Greek-style yogurt and mint. Serve immediately.

Yogurt Cheese

makes about ½ cup

Yogurt cheese, also called *labni,* is yogurt drained of its water. It has the consistency of sour cream and is sold in the refrigerator sections of Middle Eastern grocery stores. It's also easy to make your own.

1 cup plain yogurt

Spoon the yogurt into a yogurt funnel (purchased at any kitchen store) or a sieve double-lined with dampened cheesecloth and set over a deep-sided tub or bowl to catch the excess liquid. Cover with plastic wrap and leave to drain for 24 hours in the refrigerator. Transfer the resulting cheese to an airtight container. Refrigerated, the cheese will keep a few weeks.

Quince-Apple-Peach Compote

makes 3 cups

In medieval times, quince symbolized love, joy, and harmony. Spoon this luscious compote over thick slices of pound cake for the most sensual dessert since the Middle Ages.

1 cup muscatel wine
½ cup sugar
One 1-inch piece peeled fresh ginger
One 3-inch cinnamon stick
2 green cardamom pods, gently cracked
1 pound fresh quince, peeled, cored, and cut into bite-sized pieces (about 2 cups)
1 large apple, peeled, cored, and cut into bite-sized pieces
1 large peach, peeled, cored, and cut into bite-sized pieces

1. Combine the wine, sugar, ginger, cinnamon stick, and cardamom pods in a large heavy-bottomed saucepan. Bring to a boil, stirring to dissolve the sugar. Add the quince. Simmer gently over medium-low heat, stirring occasionally, for about 1 hour or until the fruit is tender and has an appetizing blush color.
2. Add the apple and peach. Cover and simmer, stirring occasionally, until the apple and peach pieces are tender, about 15 minutes. Discard the ginger, cinnamon stick, and cardamom pods.
3. This compote is delicious served at any temperature. Eat as is or spoon over sturdy cakes, cheesecake, or ice cream. Once chilled, use it to build your favorite parfait. Stored in an airtight container and chilled, the compote will stay fresh for about 5 days.

Brandied-Quince Buckle

serves 10 to 12

Buckles were most popular in the days when folks didn't count calories or worry about cholesterol. Succulent brandy-soaked quince is folded into sinful batter, and the heady result is worth throwing caution into the autumn breeze.

for the quince:

1¼ cups unsweetened apple juice

¾ cup brandy

½ cup sugar

One 3-inch cinnamon stick

1 tablespoon fresh lemon juice

1 pound fresh quince, peeled, cored, and cut into ½-inch-thick wedges (about 3 cups)

for the batter:

4 tablespoons (½ stick) butter, softened

¾ cup sugar

1 egg

2 cups sifted white all-purpose flour

2 teaspoons baking powder

½ teaspoon salt

½ cup milk

for the crunch topping:

¼ cup sugar

¼ cup firmly packed light brown sugar

⅓ cup white all-purpose flour

½ teaspoon cinnamon

4 tablespoons (½ stick) butter, cut into small cubes, plus more to grease the pan

1. Prepare the quince a day or two ahead of time. Combine the apple juice, brandy, sugar, cinnamon stick, and lemon juice in a large heavy-bottomed pot and bring to a boil. Stir in the quince. Lower the heat, cover the pot, and simmer the fruit for 45 minutes. Remove the cover and continue to simmer for an additional 30 minutes, or until the fruit is very tender and an attractive color of red. Transfer into a bowl, discard the cinnamon stick, and cool to room temperature. If you are not planning to make the buckle the same day, cover and chill. The quince will keep in its poaching liquid for up to 5 days in the refrigerator.

2. At least 2 hours before making the buckle, drain the quince in a sieve set over a bowl; reserve the poaching liquid. Blot the fruit dry on paper towels, then place the slices in an airtight container, cover, and chill for 2 to 8 hours before using.

3. Pour the reserved poaching liquid into a small saucepan and reduce to ¼ cup over medium-low heat. Set aside or refrigerate until you are ready to make the buckle.

4. Preheat the oven to 375°F. Grease a 9-inch square baking pan with butter and set aside.

5. To prepare the batter, cream the butter in a large bowl with an electric mixer. Add the sugar and beat until light and fluffy. Add the egg and blend well.

6. Sift together the flour (sifting the flour twice makes for a lighter, less dense cake), baking powder, and salt. Add a portion of the flour mixture to the butter mixture and beat well. Then beat in some of the milk. Alternating, add the rest of the flour mixture and milk, beating between each addition until smooth.

7. Toss the chilled quince wedges with the reduced poaching liquid in a small bowl until coated. Fold the fruit into the batter. Pour the batter into the prepared pan and set aside.

8. To prepare the crunch topping, combine the sugar, brown sugar, flour, and cinnamon in the bowl of a food processor and pulse to blend. Scatter the butter cubes evenly over the mixture and process to a coarse meal. Sprinkle the topping evenly over the batter.

9. Bake in the middle of the oven for 35 minutes, or until golden on top.

10. Serve warm or at room temperature. Top with a dollop of whipped cream, if desired.

Cranberry-Quince Vanilla Crunch

serves 10 to 12

Shortly after the Pilgrims arrived in Plymouth, Massachusetts, Native Americans introduced them to the mouth-puckering wild cranberry, which they sweetened with honey or maple syrup. Less than a decade later, the Pilgrims were cultivating pectin-rich quince across New England. Although no historical record exists, more likely than not, pairing the two tart fruits captured the imagination of one of those early home cooks, especially once West Indies sugar became plentiful and inexpensive.

for the quince:
1¾ to 2 pounds fresh quince, poached according to the directions on page 27
(3½ cups poached quince, drained and coarsely chopped)

for the filling:
1½ cups fresh cranberries
1½ teaspoons orange zest
½ cup firmly packed light brown sugar
½ tablespoon arrowroot

for the crunch topping:
30 vanilla wafers
⅓ cup white all-purpose flour
1 tablespoon sugar
½ teaspoon ground cinnamon
5 tablespoons chilled butter, cut into small cubes

1. Prepare the quince as directed.
2. Preheat the oven to 375°F. Coat an 8-inch square baking dish with nonstick cooking spray and set aside.

3. To prepare the filling, toss the quince, cranberries, orange zest, brown sugar, and arrowroot together in a large bowl. Spread the fruit mixture evenly in the pan.
4. To prepare the crunch topping, break up the vanilla wafers by hand into the bowl of a food processor and pulse to a fine crumb. Add the flour, sugar, and cinnamon and pulse until well blended. Scatter the butter cubes evenly over the mixture and process to a coarse meal. Sprinkle the topping evenly over the fruit mixture.
5. Bake in the middle of the oven until the top is golden brown and the juices are bubbly, 30 to 35 minutes.
6. Enjoy warm, topped with a scoop of vanilla ice cream or a dollop of whipped cream.

Sour Cherry-Quince-Almond Crisp

serves 10 to 12

Did you know that Michigan raises more tart red Montmorency cherries than anywhere else in the world? According to legend, Montmorency was a French duke who insisted on having cherries at every meal. Though the variety is now rare in its native France, every July, the beautiful Lake Michigan resort town of Traverse City holds an annual festival in its honor.

Like quince, sour cherries are tastiest when sweetened and cooked. Contrary to quinces, sour cherries have a short season, and are usually available only in June and July. Fortunately, they preserve well and can be purchased year round. The almond crisp topping is in keeping with French tradition and provides a perfect flavor balance.

No matter how much you eat, it seems impossible to decide whether this dessert is too sweet or too tart. The mystery may be what makes this attractive cobbler dangerously compelling.

for the quince:
1¾ to 2 pounds fresh quince, poached according to the directions on page 27
(3½ cups poached quince, drained and coarsely chopped)

for the filling:
1¼ to 1½ cups pitted tart cherries, drained well (see Note 1)
½ cup firmly packed light brown sugar
½ tablespoon arrowroot

for the crisp topping:
¼ cup white all-purpose flour
1 tablespoon almond meal (see Note 2)
2 tablespoons sugar
Pinch of salt

4 tablespoons (½ stick) chilled butter, cut into small cubes
2 tablespoons toasted slivered almonds

1. Prepare the quince as directed.
2. Preheat the oven to 375°F. Coat an 8-inch square baking dish lightly with nonstick cooking spray and set aside.
3. To prepare the filling, combine the quince, cherries, brown sugar, and arrowroot in a large bowl, tossing to mix. Spread the filling evenly in the prepared baking dish and set aside.
4. To prepare the crisp topping, combine the flour, almond meal, sugar, and salt in the bowl of a food processor and pulse to blend. Scatter the cold butter cubes evenly over the mixture and pulse to a coarse meal. Do not overprocess. Add the almonds and pulse just to mix. Spoon the topping evenly over the fruit filling. Do not pat firm. Left loose, the topping will make a crispier crisp.
5. Bake in the middle of the oven until the top is evenly browned and the fruit filling bubbles, about 1 hour. Cool slightly before serving with ice cream or a dollop of whipped cream.

Note 1: One 20-ounce can of cherry pie filling contains approximately 1¼ cups of cherries. Rinse and drain well before using. Dark mahogany red Morello cherries come packed in a lightly sweetened syrup. Use one 24.7-ounce jar, drained.

Note 2: Almond meal is made from finely chopped, skinned almonds. Chop 1½ tablespoons slivered, skinned almonds into a fine meal in the bowl of an electric chopper or food processor; measure again before using.

Whole-Wheat Bourbon Fruitcake

serves 10 to 12

Just a hint of bourbon rounds out this wholesome fruitcake, which is low in sugar and filled with fruit. Perfect served after a meal, or even for breakfast with your morning espresso.

for the quince:
½ to ¾ pound fresh quince, poached according to the directions on page 27
(1 to 1½ cups poached quince, drained and coarsely chopped)

for the filling:
⅓ cup raisins
¼ cup bourbon
1 cup fresh or frozen blueberries (if using frozen, thaw completely and drain well)
1 large Bosc pear, peeled, cored, and diced (1 to 1½ cups)
1 tablespoon firmly packed light brown sugar
½ teaspoon ground ginger
1 tablespoon cornstarch

for the batter:
½ cup whole-wheat flour
⅓ cup unbleached white all-purpose flour
½ cup sugar
⅓ teaspoon baking powder
¼ teaspoon salt
2 eggs
½ cup whole milk
1 teaspoon vanilla extract
2 teaspoons lemon zest

1. Prepare the quince as directed.
2. Preheat the oven to 350°F. Coat an 8-inch square pan lightly with nonstick cooking spray and set aside.
3. Combine the raisins and 2 tablespoons of the bourbon in a small bowl and set aside. The fruit will absorb the liquid while you prepare the rest of the dish.
4. To prepare the batter, combine the flours, sugar, baking powder, and salt in a mixing bowl. Using a wooden spoon, stir in the eggs, milk, the remaining 2 tablespoons bourbon, vanilla, and lemon zest; beat into a batter. Pour the batter into the prepared pan.
5. To prepare the filling, combine the quince, bourbon-soaked raisins, blueberries, pear, brown sugar, ginger, and cornstarch in a large mixing bowl; toss to blend. Spoon the fruit into the batter, distributing it evenly.
6. Bake in the middle of the oven until the batter pulls slightly away from the sides of the pan and the cake is firm, about 50 minutes. Cool on a wire rack.
7. Serve topped with whipped cream as a dessert, or cover and refrigerate. This fruitcake is a delicious way to start your day.

Pies and Tarts

Classic Quince-Apple Pie

serves 10

In Britain, quince often appears in apple pies, where it adds a unique flavor and hint of delicate pink coloring. I tried many apple varieties and returned to Julia Child's favorite, Golden Delicious. They are really the best for this pie. The crumble topping comes together with little effort using a food processor. As odd as it sounds, baking the pie in a paper bag ensures even cooking and browning.

for the quince:
2 pounds fresh quince, poached according to the directions on page 27
(3½ to 4 cups poached quince, drained)

for the crust:
One 9-inch pastry crust (recipe follows), or store-bought

for the filling:
2 Golden Delicious apples, peeled, cored, and sliced thin
2 tablespoons brandy
2 tablespoons firmly packed light brown sugar
1 tablespoon white all-purpose flour
¼ teaspoon ground nutmeg
¼ teaspoon ground cinnamon
Pinch of ground allspice

for the oatmeal crumble topping:
½ cup white all-purpose flour
⅓ cup regular oats
2 tablespoons firmly packed light brown sugar
4 tablespoon (½ stick) butter, cut into small cubes

1. Prepare the quince as directed.
2. Prepare the pie crust according to the directions on the next page. Roll it out on a floured work surface into a 10-inch circle. Slide it into a 9-inch pie plate, press gently to fit, and crimp the edges. Set aside.
3. Preheat the oven to 425°F.
4. To prepare the filling, combine the filling ingredients in a large mixing bowl and toss until mixed. Spoon the fruit mixture evenly into the uncooked pie shell.
5. To prepare the oatmeal crumble topping, combine the flour, oats, and sugar in the bowl of a food processor and blend. Scatter the butter cubes evenly over the top and process to a coarse meal. Sprinkle the topping evenly over the fruit filling.
6. Slide the pie into a large, heavy brown paper bag, fold the opening closed, and staple. Place the pie on a baking sheet and set in the oven so that the bag does not touch the top or sides of the oven. Adjust the oven racks, if necessary. Bake for 1 hour. Don't be alarmed if you "smell the bag."
7. Remove the pie from the oven. Using scissors, cut away the bag to reveal a perfectly baked pie.
8. Enjoy warm, with a scoop of ice cream or dollop of whipped cream.

Pastry Crust

makes one deep-dish or two 8- to 9-inch crusts

My laboratory science background primed me to be a baker, but pie crusts were my culinary nemesis. No matter what I did, my crusts never satisfied or added to the taste of a dessert.

Blessed be Martha Stewart. Before finding her recipe, whenever I needed a pie crust I'd buy the best-quality crust on the market and use that. Don't! This crust comes together easily with mouthwatering results. Believe me, if I can make it, you can make it!

2½ cups white all-purpose flour

3 tablespoons sugar

½ pound (2 sticks) unsalted butter, chilled and cut into small pieces

2 egg yolks

¼ cup ice water, plus more if needed

1. Combine the flour and sugar in the bowl of a large food processor. Scatter the butter evenly over the top and process to a coarse meal, about 20 seconds.
2. Lightly beat the egg yolks in a small mixing bowl, then whisk in the ice water. Slowly pour the egg mixture into the dough, pulsing, until the dough holds together without being wet or sticky. This should not take more than 30 seconds. To test, squeeze a small amount together. If it is crumbly, add more ice water, 1 tablespoon at a time.
3. Divide the dough into two equal balls. Flatten each ball into a disk on a floured work surface and wrap in plastic. Chill in the refrigerator for at least 1 hour. Dough may kept in the refrigerator for a few days or frozen for up to 1 month.

Creamy Quince Mascarpone Pie

serves 10

Quince is a classic holiday fruit, and this taste blend—something between a squash and an apple pie—is dreamy. It's so light and tangy, you may never go back to pumpkin again.

for the quince:

¾ pound fresh quince, peeled, cored, and diced (about 2 cups)

4 cups water

for the crust:

One 9-inch pastry crust (page 149), or store-bought

for the filling:

1 cup firmly packed light brown sugar

2 eggs

1 teaspoon ground cinnamon

1 teaspoon ground ginger

½ teaspoon ground nutmeg

¼ teaspoon ground cloves

¼ teaspoon salt

1 teaspoon fresh lemon juice

½ teaspoon vanilla extract

1 cup mascarpone cheese

1. This pie requires the quince to be puréed, similar to store-bought pumpkin or squash purée. Quince purée may be refrigerated for up to a couple of days before using, so consider doing this step in advance. To prepare the quince, combine the fruit and water in a heavy-bottomed medium-sized pot and bring to a boil. Lower

the heat and simmer uncovered, stirring occasionally, for 1 hour, or until the quince is very soft. Very little liquid will remain. Cool for 10 minutes. While it is still quite warm, purée the cooked fruit and remaining liquid until very smooth. The purée will look and smell like applesauce. Measure 1 cup and set aside. (If you have extra purée, consider making Open-Faced Quince Sandwiches, page 42.)

2. Prepare the pie crust according to the directions on page 149. Roll it out on a floured work surface into a 10-inch circle. Slide it into a 9-inch pie plate, press gently to fit, and crimp the edges. Set aside.

3. Preheat the oven to 350°F.

4. Beat 1 cup quince purée and the brown sugar in a large bowl with an electric mixer. Add the eggs, cinnamon, ginger, nutmeg, cloves, salt, lemon juice, vanilla, and mascarpone; mix well. Pour the batter into the unbaked crust.

5. Place the pie on a baking sheet and bake in the middle of the oven for 1 hour, or until a knife inserted in the center comes out clean. Cool on a wire rack. Serve at room temperature topped with whipped cream, if desired.

Quick and Easy Ricotta Tart with Quince

serves 12

I searched for a to-die-for ricotta pie recipe that lived up to its claim of being easy and fail-proof. I found it offered by Elisa Mazzaferro-Rosenberg of Fort Collins, Colorado (*Bon Appetit*, March 2003). Her recipe is a version from her grandmother Elsie, but ricotta pie is traditional on both sides of her Italian family. Slightly adapted and paired with quince, this tart has become a tradition in my family, too. Thank you, Elisa!

for the quince:

1½ to 1¾ pounds fresh quince, poached according to the directions on page 27
(3 to 3½ cups poached quince, drained, patted dry with paper towels,
and chilled in an airtight container for at least 2 hours before using)

for the crust:

One 9-inch pie crust (page 149) (do not substitute store-bought)

for the filling:

2 cups (one 15- to 16-ounce container) ricotta cheese (preferably whole-milk)
⅓ cup (3 ounces) cream cheese, room temperature
1 tablespoon cornstarch
1 teaspoon vanilla extract
½ cup sugar
1½ teaspoons orange zest
2 eggs

1. Prepare the quince as directed.
2. Prepare the tart crust according to the directions on page 149. Roll it out on a floured work surface to fit an 8-inch square baking pan. Press the dough firmly into the pan; crimp the edges, if necessary; and set aside.
3. Preheat the oven to 350°F.
4. To prepare the filling, beat the ricotta, cream cheese, cornstarch, and vanilla in a large bowl with an electric mixer until blended. Beat in the sugar, orange zest, and eggs.
5. Arrange the quince wedges in a single layer in the bottom of the dough-covered pan. Pour the filling evenly over the top.
6. Bake in the middle of the oven for 1 hour, or until the tart is firm, puffed, and golden on top. Cool completely before cutting into individual serving-sized squares.

Buttery Almond-Quince Phyllo Tarts

makes 8 tarts

In 1570 Pope Pius V hosted a spectacular banquet that featured, as its pièce de résistance, a pastry that required "one quince per pastry." My version of the pope's masterpiece nestles succulent poached quince wedges in feathery phyllo. The phyllo tends to absorb moisture from the atmosphere, so these tarts are best eaten the day they are prepared.

for the quince:
1½ pounds fresh quince, poached according to the directions on page 27
(about 24 ½-inch-thick wedges, drained and patted dry with paper towels)

for the filling:
1½ tablespoons unsalted butter, softened

2 tablespoons sugar, plus more to sprinkle

½ teaspoon ground cinnamon

½ cup almond meal (see Note 1)

1 egg yolk

for the pastry:
10 sheets phyllo dough, room temperature

6 tablespoons clarified butter or ghee, melted (see Note 2)

to finish:
2 tablespoons quince or red currant jelly, melted

Confectioners' sugar, optional

1. Prepare the quince as directed.
2. Preheat the oven to 375°F.
3. To prepare the filling, cream the butter in a small bowl using an electric mixer until light yellow and fluffy. Add the sugar and blend well. Beat in the cinnamon, almond meal, and egg yolk. Set the batter aside.
4. Unwrap the phyllo dough and remove 10 sheets. Rewrap the remainder and reserve it for another use. Place the phyllo near the flat work surface where you will assemble the phyllo packages. Cover immediately with a double layer of plastic wrap and a clean, dampened kitchen towel to prevent the dough from drying out.
5. To assemble, lay 1 phyllo sheet on the flat work surface. Using a pastry brush and working quickly, brush the sheet with clarified butter, then sprinkle it lightly with sugar. Place a second sheet on top, brush it with ghee, and add a sprinkle of sugar; repeat until you have layered 5 sheets of dough.
6. Cut the phyllo stack in half lengthwise with a sharp knife. The result will be two 9 × 6½-inch rectangles; cut each rectangle in half lengthwise to make four 4½ × 3¼-inch sections. Spread ⅛ portion of filling down the center of each section, leaving 1 inch around the edges of each section without filling.
7. Slice the quince wedges lengthwise into two ¼-inch-thick slices. (You will have a total of about 48 slices). Lay 6 slices down the center of a phyllo rectangle, like cascading tiles. Using a sharp knife, trim the two uncut edges of the rectangle to even, if necessary; fold the sides in and the top and bottom over the quince slices, partially enclosing the fruit into a tidy package (see picture). Repeat the process until all 8 tarts are assembled.
8. Place the tarts on a baking tray lined with parchment paper. Brush the phyllo crust with a little melted ghee and sprinkle lightly with sugar. This will help the phyllo bake golden and sparkly. Finally, brush the exposed quince slices with melted jelly and bake in the middle of the oven for 15 minutes, or until golden.
9. Cool on a wire rack. Dust each tart lightly with confectioners' sugar, if using. Consume the same day.

Note 1: Use store-bought ghee (butter with milk solids extracted) or prepare your own. Melt 6 tablespoons unsalted butter in a small saucepan over low heat or in a microwave. Let it stand until the white milk solids have settled. Pour off and reserve the clear (clarified) butter. Discard the solids. Melt the clarified butter again before using, if necessary.

Note 2: Almond meal is made from finely chopped, skinned almonds. Chop a rounded ½ cup slivered, skinned almonds into a fine meal in the bowl of an electric chopper or food processor; measure again before using.

Quince Clafouti

serves 10

Light, rich, and creamy, this pudding-like dessert is a French classic. As long as you have poached quince in the refrigerator, it assembles quickly and cooks fail-proof. Sublime when served slightly warm or just at room temperature.

for the quince:
1¾ to 2 pounds fresh quince, poached according to the directions on page 27
(3½ cups poached quince, drained, patted dry with paper towels,
and chilled in an airtight container for at least 2 hours before using)

for the pan:
1 tablespoon unsalted butter, room temperature

for the custard:
⅓ cup plus 1 tablespoon sugar
3 extra-large eggs, room temperature
6 tablespoons white all-purpose flour
1½ cups heavy cream
1 teaspoon lemon zest
2 teaspoons vanilla extract
2 tablespoons apricot brandy
¼ teaspoon salt

to finish:
Confectioners' sugar

Pies and Tarts

157

1. Prepare the quince as directed.
2. Preheat the oven to 375°F. Butter a 9-inch round baking pan (no substitutions). Sprinkle the bottom and sides of the pan with 1 tablespoon of the sugar. Set aside.
3. To prepare the custard, beat the eggs and the remaining ⅓ cup sugar in a large bowl with an electric mixer on medium-high speed until pale yellow, light, and fluffy. This important step takes 3 minutes. Add the flour, cream, lemon zest, vanilla, brandy, and salt. Mix at low speed until combined. Set aside to stand for 10 minutes.
4. Slice the chilled wedges lengthwise so they are of uniform thickness, if necessary. Arrange the slices in a fan or wheel pattern in a single layer in the prepared pan. Pour the custard evenly over the fruit.
5. Bake in the middle of the oven for 35 to 40 minutes, or until the top is golden brown and the custard is firm. Cool on a wire rack for 10 minutes. Loosen the sides from the pan with a knife, place a large plate over the pan, flip upside down, and gently pat the bottom to loosen and release whole. Place a serving dish on the exposed fruit layer and flip again, so the browned custard top is showing.
6. Dust with confectioners' sugar, slice, and serve slightly warm or at room temperature. Best served the day of preparation; the custard tends to firm and crack when held over.

Afternoon Tea

Scones with Quince

makes 8 scones

I learned to make scones in home economics class in eighth grade, and I've been using this childhood recipe ever since. Adding supple, slightly sweetened poached quince was a natural.

The result is a heartwarming quick bread elegant enough for the poshest tea rooms yet homey enough for country hearths. Brew a fresh pot of Earl Grey tea and serve the scones right-from-the-oven warm, lavished with butter.

for the quince:

½ pound fresh quince, poached according to the directions on page 27

(1 cup poached quince, drained, coarsely chopped, patted dry with paper towels, and chilled in an airtight container for at least 2 hours before using)

for the scones:

2 cups white all-purpose flour, plus more for rolling

¼ cup sugar

3 teaspoons baking powder

¼ teaspoon salt

4 tablespoons (½ stick) butter, cut into small cubes and softened

1 egg, slightly beaten

⅔ cup evaporated milk

Coarse sugar

1. Prepare the quince as directed.
2. Preheat the oven to 400°F.
3. Combine 2 cups of the flour with the sugar, baking powder, and salt in a large bowl and mix to blend. Using a fork or pastry blender, cut in the butter until the mixture is crumbly.

4. Whisk together the egg and milk in a small bowl until well blended. Add the milk mixture to the flour mixture all at once and stir until just moistened. Fold in the quince.
5. Turn the dough out onto a floured work surface. Knead gently a few times, then shape the dough into an 8-inch circle, about 1 inch thick. Place the circle on a baking sheet lined with parchment paper. Cut it into 8 wedges (do not separate), and sprinkle the top with coarse sugar.
6. Bake in the middle of the oven for 15 to 20 minutes, or until golden brown.
7. Enjoy warm, swiped with butter and your favorite quince preserve, of course.

Quince Coffee Cake

makes 1 cake

Two medium quinces spruce up the ubiquitous pound cake. The result is a moist offering with subtle fruit flavor and eye-catching appeal. This recipe is so delicious that I recommend baking two cakes; eat one and freeze the other for the holidays.

for the quince:

2 cups water

¾ cup sugar

2 teaspoons fresh lemon juice

One 3-inch cinnamon stick

1 pound fresh quince, peeled, cored, and cut into ½-inch-thick wedges (about 3 cups)

for the batter:

1¾ cups cake flour

¼ teaspoon ground cinnamon

¼ teaspoon salt

¼ pound (1 stick) unsalted butter, softened

1½ cups sugar

1 egg yolk

3 eggs

½ cup heavy cream

1 teaspoon vanilla extract

1. The quince may be poached up to 3 days ahead of preparing the cake. Combine the water, sugar, lemon juice, cinnamon stick, and quince in a large heavy-bottomed pot. Heat to a simmer, cover, and continue to gently simmer for 2 to 2½ hours, or until the quince turns a deep red color. This long-cook method of poaching quince maximizes the fruit's color transformation.

2. Remove from the heat, discard the cinnamon stick, cool to room temperature, and then chill until cold, about 2 hours; chilling will firm the fruit. Drain the chilled fruit through a sieve and pat dry on paper towels. Cover and chill again for at least 3 hours and up to 3 days before using.
3. Preheat the oven to 350°F. Line a 9-inch cake pan with parchment paper and set aside.
4. Sift together the flour, cinnamon, and salt twice. Set aside in a bowl.
5. Beat the butter and sugar in a large bowl using an electric mixer until light and frothy. Add the egg yolk and whole eggs, one at a time, beating for at least 1 minute after each addition. Then add half of the flour mixture and all of the cream. Beat until just combined. Add the remaining flour mixture and the vanilla. Beat again until just combined. Fold the quince into the batter and spread the batter evenly in the pan.
6. Bake in the middle of the oven for 1 hour 10 minutes, or until a toothpick inserted in the center comes out clean and the top is golden brown.
7. Cool on a wire rack for 20 minutes. Turn the cake out onto the rack to cool completely. Serve with coffee or tea; this cake stands alone.

Katayif Pastry Stuffed with Quince and Mascarpone Cheese

serves 12

This rich, distinctively Middle Eastern-influenced dessert has a subtle nutty-cheese-quince center. Served dripping in lemony-sweet syrup, it is one of the most exotic recipes in the collection. For those unfamiliar with Middle Eastern pastries, katayif dough is simply shredded phyllo dough that looks and feels like extra-thin angel hair pasta. In my grandmother's day, moistened shredded wheat was a common substitute.

for the syrup:

1 cup sugar

¾ cup water

1 tablespoon fresh lemon juice (for a more exotic aroma and flavor,
substitute ¼ teaspoon orange flower or rose water, preferably French)

for the filling:

1 cup mascarpone cheese, room temperature

¼ cup finely chopped walnuts or pistachio nuts, plus 2 tablespoons for garnish

½ cup Quince-Orange Marmalade (page 120) (or substitute any sweet quince preserve)

for the pastry:

1 pound (1 package) katayif dough (see Note)

½ pound (2 sticks) unsalted butter, melted

1. To prepare the syrup, combine the sugar and water in a saucepan. Bring to a boil, stirring to dissolve the sugar, then lower the heat and simmer for 15 minutes; the syrup will thicken slightly. Stir in the lemon juice and set aside to cool.

2. To prepare the filling, combine the mascarpone, ¼ cup of the nuts, and the marmalade in a small bowl; set the filling aside.

3. Preheat the oven to 375°F.

4. Open the package of katayif dough. In a large mixing bowl, pull the dough strands apart by hand until separated completely. Pour the melted butter over the dough and toss (with your hands) until the dough is evenly buttered. This is fun! Don't be intimidated. You can't make a mistake.

5. Arrange two-thirds of the dough evenly over the bottom of a 9-inch square baking pan. Spread the filling mixture evenly over the dough. Then cover the filling with the remaining dough.

6. Cover with foil and bake in the middle of the oven for 30 minutes. Remove the foil and bake for an additional 20 minutes, or until the top is golden brown.

7. Remove from the oven and immediately pour the cooled syrup evenly over the warm pastry. Garnish with the remaining 2 tablespoons chopped nuts. Cover with foil again and let stand for about 20 minutes before serving. Cut into squares and serve warm. Refrigerate any leftovers.

Note: Katayif dough is sold in the freezer section of Middle Eastern grocers. Apollo brand Shredded Fillo Dough (spelled *kataif*) is the easiest to find.

Caramelized Quince Upside-Down Cake

serves 10

Caramel sauce and almond-flavored cake complement quince beautifully. The combination offers a delicious new twist on an old-time favorite.

for the quince:
1 pound fresh quince, poached according to the directions on page 27
(about sixteen ½-inch-thick wedges, drained, patted dry with paper towels,
and chilled in an airtight container for at least 2 hours before using)

for the caramel sauce:
¾ cup firmly packed light brown sugar
2 tablespoons water
4 tablespoons (½ stick) butter, plus more to grease the pan

for the batter:
¼ pound (1 stick) unsalted butter, softened
½ cup sugar
2 eggs
½ teaspoon vanilla extract
½ cup white all-purpose flour
1 teaspoon baking powder
½ cup almond meal (see Note)

1. Prepare the quince as directed.
2. Preheat the oven to 325°F. Lightly butter an 8-inch round cake pan and set aside.
3. To prepare the caramel sauce, combine the brown sugar, water, and 4 tablespoons of the butter in a small saucepan. Bring to a boil, stirring until the sugar is dissolved,

then boil for about 3 minutes, or until the ingredients blend and the sauce thickens slightly. Remove from the heat and set aside.

4. To prepare the batter, beat the softened butter and sugar in a large bowl with an electric mixer until light and fluffy. Add the eggs and vanilla; beat well. Add the flour, baking powder, and almond meal. Beat the batter on high speed for 6 minutes (no skimping on time, please), scraping down the sides of the bowl periodically, until the batter is well combined.

5. Reheat and stir the caramel sauce if it is too firm, then spoon three-quarters of it into the prepared pan; swirl to cover the bottom of the pan evenly. Set the remaining sauce aside.

6. Slice the chilled quince wedges lengthwise into ¼- to ⅜-inch-thick slices. Arrange the slices in the pan in a single layer, in a concentric circle beginning from the center and radiating out to the edge of the pan, like a pinwheel. Spoon the batter evenly on top. Often the caramel sauce will creep up the side of the pan; don't worry, that's perfectly normal.

7. Bake in the middle of the oven for 30 minutes, or until golden brown on top and a skewer inserted in the center comes out clean. Remove to a wire rack. Cool for 10 minutes. Run a knife around the circumference of the pan to loosen the cake, cover with a serving platter, flip quickly, and gently pat the bottom to release the cake. Rewarm the remaining caramel sauce if it is too firm, then spoon it over the top. After baking, the quince will be a gorgeous brick color and very tender.

8. Serve individual slices topped with a dollop of whipped cream.

Note: Almond meal is made from finely chopped, skinned almonds. Chop a rounded ½ cup slivered, skinned almonds into a fine meal in the bowl of an electric chopper or food processor; measure again before using.

Quince Linzer Cookies

Homemade ruby-red quince jelly sparkles as the bull's-eye of these festive butter cookies. They taste as amazing as they look.

2 cups plus 2 tablespoons cake flour
½ teaspoon salt
½ pound (2 sticks) unsalted butter, softened
1 cup sugar
2 egg yolks
1 teaspoon vanilla extract
1½ cups Quince Jelly (page 128)
Confectioners' sugar

1. Sift together the flour and salt into a mixing bowl. Set aside.
2. Beat the butter in a large bowl with an electric mixer on high speed for about 5 minutes, or until pale yellow and fluffy. The butter needs to be whipped for a long time; otherwise the batter will be too stiff when chilled. Add the sugar and beat at medium-high speed until very pale, 2 to 3 minutes. Scrape down the sides of the bowl and beat in the egg yolks and vanilla until well blended. Slowly add the flour mixture until the batter collects into a dough.
3. Shape the dough into a log. Wrap in plastic wrap and refrigerate until well chilled, at least 2½ hours. Dough may be kept refrigerated up to 3 days.
4. Preheat the oven to 350°F and line two cookie sheets with parchment paper.
5. On a lightly floured work surface, roll the dough out into a ⅛- to ¼-inch-thick sheet. Use a circular cookie cutter to cut 3-inch rounds. Place half of the rounds 1 inch apart on the cookie sheets. Spread each evenly with a thin layer of quince jelly. If the jelly is too firm to spread evenly, warming it slightly should do the trick. Then, using a 1½-inch circular cookie cutter, cut a hole in the center of the

remaining rounds to form rings. Place one ring on top of each jelly-layered round to make an open sandwich cookie. Repeat the assembly process, rolling all the dough and scraps, until all of the dough has been used. Substitute a linzer cookie cutter for the circular cookie cutters, if desired.

6. Bake in the middle of the oven until golden, 10 to 12 minutes, depending on the thickness. Remove from the oven and cool for about 5 minutes before transferring them to a wire rack.

7. When cooled completely, sprinkle lightly with confectioners' sugar.

Quintessential
Favorites

German Quince Pancake

My daughter saw a German apple pancake featured in *Cooking Light* (August 2008) and suggested I adapt it for quince. Thank you, Talin! With this recipe, the collection benefits from an all-in-one breakfast treat that's sinfully like fruit-topped French toast and flan—for less than 200 calories per serving.

for the quince:
¾ pound fresh quince, poached according to the directions on page 27
(about twelve ½-inch-thick wedges, drained and patted dry with paper towels)

for the batter:
½ cup white all-purpose flour
½ teaspoon baking powder
1 tablespoon sugar
Pinch of salt
Pinch of ground nutmeg
1 cup egg substitute
1 cup fat-free milk
2 tablespoons butter, melted
1 teaspoon vanilla extract

for the quince mixture:
½ cup sugar
½ teaspoon ground cinnamon
Pinch of ground nutmeg

to finish:
Confectioners' sugar

1. Prepare the quince as directed.
2. To prepare the batter, combine the flour, baking powder, sugar, salt, and nutmeg; stir to mix. Vigorously whisk together the egg substitute, milk, butter, and vanilla in a mixing bowl until well blended. Stir the egg mixture into the flour mixture and beat by hand until blended. Let stand for 30 minutes.
3. Preheat the oven to 425°F. Coat the bottom and sides of a 10-inch ovenproof skillet with nonstick cooking spray. Set aside.
4. To prepare the quince mixture, combine ¼ cup of the sugar with the cinnamon and nutmeg in a small bowl. Sprinkle it evenly over the bottom and sides of the pan. With a sharp knife, cut the quince wedges lengthwise into ¼-inch-thick slices. Arrange the quince slices in a pinwheel pattern on top. Sprinkle the remaining ¼ cup sugar over the fruit. Place the pan on the stove top and cook over medium heat until the mixture bubbles, about 5 minutes.
5. Slowly pour the batter over the quince. Bake in the middle of the oven for 15 minutes; lower the oven temperature to 375°F and bake until the center is set, another 10 to 15 minutes.
6. Let the pancake stand for a few minutes before serving. To serve, loosen the edges and gently slide the pancake onto a large serving dish. Dust with confectioners' sugar, cut into wedges, and serve warm.

Grilled Quince and Cheese Sandwiches

makes 1 sandwich; multiply as needed

For best results, use a panini press to make these sandwiches; the ridged grill will mark the bread with attractive grill strips, and the quince paste and cheese will blend into a rich, decadent melt. Serve with a tossed green salad to massage your guilt. If guilt is not a concern, pour yourself a jigger of sherry or port.

2 thin slices (2 ounces) blue cheese, Gruyere, fresh white Mexican or Syrian cheese, or Haloumi (see Note)
2 thick slices whole-grain bread
Fresh mint leaves, optional
2 thin slices (2 ounces) Quince Paste (page 32)
Extra-virgin olive oil or softened butter

1. Preheat the panini press, if using. Lay the cheese in a single layer over one slice of bread. Arrange the mint leaves, if using, and quince paste slices on the cheese, and place the second slice of bread on top. Press to flatten.
2. Brush the outer surfaces of the bread lightly with olive oil or butter. Grill the sandwich over medium-high heat. If using a skillet, press down occasionally with the back of a spatula. Cook until the cheese has melted and the bread is toasted golden brown and crispy, about 3 minutes per side.
3. Serve with a tossed green salad for a lunchtime or light dinner treat.

Note: Haloumi cheese originated on the island of Cyprus and is a favorite grilling or melting cheese of the Mediterranean and Middle East. It's a white, semi-soft sheep's-milk cheese, or a blend of sheep's-milk and goat's-milk cheese, with a mild, salty flavor that balances with my not-too-sweet quince paste fabulously. Fresh mint accents this sandwich perfectly.

White Pizza with Quince, Prosciutto, Asiago Cheese, and Chives

serves 6

Like quince, flatbread pizzas have a long tradition in the Middle Eastern kitchen. Crisp, baked prosciutto accents succulent, roasted quince, especially when set on healthy whole-wheat crust and held together with slightly tangy Asiago cheese.

for the quince:

½ pound fresh quince, poached according to the directions on page 27

(1 cup poached quince, drained, coarsely chopped, and patted dry with paper towels)

for the dough:

2 pounds store-bought fresh or frozen wheat pizza dough, proofed according to
the package directions, or homemade (ingredients follow)

1¼ cups warm water (105°F to 115°F)

1 package (¼ ounce) active dry yeast

1 teaspoon sugar

2 tablespoons extra-virgin olive oil, plus more to grease the bowl and baking sheet

2 teaspoons salt

1¾ cups whole-wheat flour

1½ to 2 cups white all-purpose flour, or more as needed

for the topping:

2 tablespoons extra-virgin olive oil

1½ to 2 cups shredded Asiago cheese (or a combination of Asiago and Parmigiano-Reggiano)

4 thin slices (2 ounces) prosciutto di Parma

1 to 2 tablespoons snipped fresh chives

1. Prepare the quince as directed.
2. If using proofed store-bought dough, skip to Step 4. If making your own dough, whisk ¼ cup of the warm water with the yeast and sugar in a large bowl or the bowl of a stand mixer. Cover with plastic wrap and let stand until foamy, about 10 minutes.
3. Mount the bowl in the mixer and attach the dough hook. (This dough is also easy to make by hand.) Add the remaining 1 cup warm water, 2 tablespoons of the olive oil, and the salt and wheat flour to the yeast mixture and mix until smooth. Gradually add the white flour, stirring, until the dough comes away from the sides of the bowl.
4. Turn the dough out onto a floured work surface and knead until it is smooth and elastic, about 10 minutes. Add extra flour as needed to keep the dough from being too sticky. Shape the dough into a ball and place it in a large bowl greased lightly with olive oil. Turn the ball once to coat it completely with oil. Cover with plastic wrap and let stand in a warm place until doubled in size, 1 to 1½ hours.
5. Turn the proofed dough out onto a floured work surface and punch down. Shape the dough into an oval; roll into a 14-inch oval about ⅜-inch thick with a heavy rolling pin. Carefully slide the round onto a lightly greased pizza or baking sheet; crimp the edges to fit the pan, if necessary; and set aside.
6. Preheat the oven to 450°F.
7. Brush the dough round lightly with olive oil; top evenly with cheese. Remove any large sections of fat from the prosciutto, snip into 1-inch ribbons with kitchen shears, and then distribute over the cheese. Do the same with the quince pieces; scatter the top with chives.
8. Bake in the middle of the oven for 15 minutes, or until the cheese is melted and the crust is golden brown.
9. Slice and serve at once accompanied with lightly dressed salad greens and a glass of white wine.

Baked Orange-Glazed Quinces with Crème Anglaise

The culinary experience of baking quince begins with the appetizing aroma that will permeate your home within minutes of popping the fruit into the oven. The experience ends with an unforgettable mouthful of succulent fruit dripping in sweet orange glaze and a nut crunch and laced with vanilla-infused crème anglaise topping. Oh, so good!

for the quince:
4 medium or large fresh quinces

for the stuffing:
⅓ cup raisins

2 tablespoons Quince Jam (page 124), or substitute apricot preserves or orange marmalade

for the syrup:
2 tablespoon firmly packed light brown sugar

2 tablespoons honey

¼ cup water

2 tablespoons fresh orange juice

1 teaspoon orange zest

1 tablespoon butter

for the crème anglaise:
½ cup half-and-half

½ cup heavy cream

One 1½-inch piece vanilla bean or 1 teaspoon vanilla extract (see Note 1)

2 egg yolks, lightly beaten
2 tablespoons sugar

to finish:
4 teaspoons apricot brandy
¼ cup lightly toasted slivered almonds (see Note 2)
Grated fresh nutmeg

1. Bake the whole quinces according to the directions on page 29. Remove from the oven and cool enough to handle. Do not turn the oven off.
2. Prepare the stuffing, syrup, and crème anglaise while the quinces are baking.
3. To prepare the stuffing, mix the raisins and preserves together in a small bowl; set aside.
4. To prepare the syrup, combine the brown sugar, honey, water, orange juice, orange zest, and butter in a small saucepan. Bring to a boil, stirring to dissolve the sugar. Lower the heat and simmer for 3 minutes. Set aside.
5. To prepare the crème anglaise, combine the half-and-half and cream in a small heavy-bottomed saucepan. Split the vanilla bean, if using, in half lengthwise and scrape the tiny seeds from the inside of the bean into the cream; then drop in the bean. Or, add the vanilla extract. Whisk and heat over medium heat until just simmering (do not boil). Remove from the heat, cover with plastic wrap placed directly on the surface of the cream mixture, and steep for 15 minutes. Remove the vanilla bean, if using.
6. Whisk together the egg yolks and sugar in a mixing bowl until well blended. Remove the plastic wrap from the cream mixture and slowly whisk the cream mixture into the eggs, then return the cream to the saucepan.
7. Cook over low heat, stirring constantly, until the mixture thickens and lightly coats the back of a spoon, about 5 minutes. It's done when your finger leaves a clear trail on the back of the spoon. Strain through a fine sieve into a bowl, cover with plastic wrap placed directly on top to prevent a skin forming, and let stand. If not using immediately, chill. The crème anglaise will keep for about a week in the refrigerator.
8. To assemble, cut each whole baked quince in half and core with a sharp knife, melon baller, or peach pitter. Spoon an equal amount of stuffing into the

hollowed-out center of each half, then set each half in a shallow baking dish lined with foil.

9. Spoon the syrup over the stuffed quinces, cover the pan with foil, and bake until the fruit is very tender, 30 to 45 minutes; baste with syrup from the pan at least once during the baking time. Cool for about 10 minutes before serving.

10. Set each warm quince half on an individual dessert plate. To finish, top with ½ teaspoon of the apricot brandy, a sprinkle of almonds, a generous drizzle of crème anglaise, and a light dusting of nutmeg.

Note 1: At the outset of my journey to expand the repertoire of quince dishes, my instinct immediately paired quince with vanilla, thinking it would be a heavenly match. It's not. When cooked together, the subtle flavor of quince is quickly overpowered by the boldness of vanilla. But drizzling vanilla crème on top satisfies the love of both flavors—an ideal compromise.

Note 2: Bake the slivered almonds at 350°F for about 8 minutes, tossing once during the cooking time.

Grand Marnier Ice Cream with Bits of Quince

makes 1½ pints

So delicious. So easy. So gourmet! This ice cream has it all. You will need about ¼ pound quince paste. Prepare the paste at home (page 32) or buy it. Quince paste is sold by many high-end grocers, especially those specializing in cheeses.

2 eggs

1 egg yolk

2 cups heavy cream

1 cup whole milk

¾ cup sugar

one 1 × 3-inch strip orange rind

2 teaspoons Grand Marnier liqueur

½ cup finely diced Quince Paste (page 32)

Coarsely chopped walnuts, optional

1. Whisk together the eggs and egg yolk in a large mixing bowl until pale yellow, about 3 minutes. Add the cream, milk, sugar, and orange rind, whisking briskly to blend.
2. Pour the mixture into a medium-sized heavy-bottomed saucepan. Cook over medium heat, stirring constantly, until the mixture thickens to lightly coat the back of a spoon; a thermometer should register between 170° and 180°F. If you have a double boiler, cook this custard in the top boiler set over 1 inch of simmering water.
3. Transfer to a bowl, cover with a layer of plastic wrap placed directly on the surface of the custard, and cool for 20 minutes to room temperature before transferring to the refrigerator to chill.

4. When you are ready to freeze the custard, strain it to remove any lumps and discard the orange rind. Stir in the liqueur. Process the custard in an ice cream maker, according to the manufacturer's instructions, for 25 to 30 minutes. Using the ingredient spout, add the diced quince bits during the last 5 minutes of mixing. Transfer the ice cream into an airtight container and place in the freezer for at least 2 hours before serving.
5. Serve sprinkled with walnuts, if using.

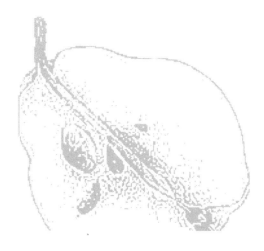

Quince-Infused Spirits
Grappa and Vodka

makes about 1 pint

Made worldwide, but especially throughout the wine-growing regions of southern Europe, the colorless brandy known as grappa is steeped with fruit and spices into an opaque dessert elixir called *ratafia*. The process begins with grappa, the clear alcohol made from surplus wine grapes, which is distilled at the end of the wine-making season.

Originating from the Latin phrase *rata fiat*, meaning "to ratify," ratafia has long been served as a celebratory cocktail to toast the close of a business deal or the signing of a treaty. In keeping with this tradition, my photo team and I toasted the successful conclusion of the photo shoot for this book with jiggers of Quince-Infused Grappa.

Infusing grappa with quince is easy. Even a cheap grappa, which is little more than high-octane firewater, transforms into a tawny cordial that tastes as warm and comforting as it looks. Serve as the finale to a home-cooked meal or sip straight on a chilly winter evening while reading a book by the fire.

QUINCE-INFUSED GRAPPA

½ to ¾ pound fresh quince, peels left on but visible blemishes removed, cored,
and grated or chopped (about 2 cups)
2 cups grappa or clear brandy (see Note)
1 cup sugar
Two 3-inch pieces vanilla bean, freshly cut at the ends (do not split lengthwise)
6 coriander seeds
2 cardamom pods, gently cracked

Prepare as directed in steps 1–5 on the following pages.

SPICED QUINCE VODKA

Vodka is the chameleon of distilled liquors. It absorbs introduced flavors effortlessly and makes them its own.

I serve this heady spirit chilled freezer-cold as an aperitif. It's guaranteed to stimulate conversation as well as the appetite.

½ to ¾ pound fresh quince, peel left on but visible blemishes removed, cored,
and grated or chopped (about 2 cups)
2 cups vodka
1 cup sugar
3 whole cloves
One 3-inch cinnamon stick
Pinch of ground mace
½ teaspoon almond extract

1. Mix the ingredients together in a clean wide-mouth 1-liter Mason jar or glass jar with an airtight cover. Cover tightly and shake vigorously until the sugar is completely dissolved. Make sure the fruit is completely immersed in liquid. If not, remove some fruit or add more spirit until the fruit is covered. If you don't own a pretty decanter, consider saving the liquor bottle and cap. (Many grappa bottles are beautifully shaped and will show off the rose-hued spirit beautifully when the time comes.)

2. Label the jar; jot down the recipe, the date of preparation, and the date five weeks later. That's when the liqueur will be ready to strain and drink. Once labeled, stash the jar in a cool dark place, such as a cupboard or pantry closet; temperatures ranging from 50°F to 75°F are best. Put it where you'll see it often, so you will be reminded to shake it.

3. Return to it every day for the first week or two and give it a shake to help the alcohol maceration of the fruit, and every week or so after that for approximately five weeks. Over time the contents of the jar will darken, and it may not look appetizing or drinkable. Don't be discouraged. This is the ugly-duckling phase; your swan is coming!

4. After five weeks of steeping, strain through a sieve lined with two layers of dampened cheesecloth. Press the fruit firmly with a potato masher or the back of a large spoon to harvest every last drop.
5. Transfer the liquid to a clean airtight decanter or glass bottle. Savor your homemade ratafia immediately. It will keep indefinitely, but I don't think that will be a concern.

Note: Grappa is traditionally Italian, and most grappa sold in the United States is imported from Europe. A Pisco from Chile or Peru can be substituted. Clear Creek in Oregon is the premier grappa producer in the lower forty-eight states.

Quince Vodka Toddy

serves 1

Warm up a winter eve with this comforting toddy.

2 ounces Spiced Quince Vodka
6 ounces water
Fresh lemon juice

Combine the vodka and water in a mug. Place in the microwave and heat for 2 minutes on high. Serve hot with a squeeze of fresh lemon juice.

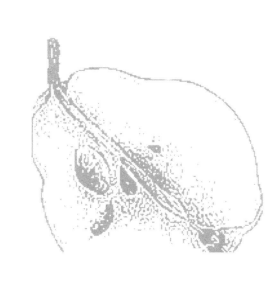

KITCHEN TOOLS

A carpenter's job is easier with the right tools on hand, and the same applies to cooking with quince. Likely your kitchen is already equipped with the basic items used in the collection, and even many listed in the following sections under "Quincing Tools" and "Canning Tools." However, a few are uncommon, such as the hard-to-find peach pitter, a must-have for coring quince. Some of the canning supplies will also make your quincing adventure significantly easier. None will break the bank, and if not available locally, they can be purchased from my website or from vendors listed in SOURCES.

Quincing Tools

> Food scale that measures up to 5 pounds
> Wide, swivel-bladed potato peeler
> Sharp paring knife
> Sharp 6-inch multipurpose knife
> Sharp 8- to 10-inch chef's knife (Furi's Rachael Ray Gusto-Grip fruit knife is my favorite)
> Peach pitter, aka Fresno Armenian Ladies' Kitchen Widget (see SOURCES)

Canning Tools

Cheesecloth
Candy and deep-fry ruler thermometer
Foam skimmer
Nonreactive ladle*
Wide-mouth canning funnel
Self-sealing glass canning jars with lids and screw tops approved for home-canning (always use new lids)
Thin plastic spatula, used to release air bubbles in your filled jars before sealing
Magnetic lid wand, or tongs
Water-bath canner, or jumbo enamelware or stainless steel pot with a tight-fitting lid
Wire jar rack
Jar lifter

A peach pitter is a tool designed specifically for removing the thready centers around the pit of a peach and is used almost exclusively by workers in canning factories. It's a 6-inch-long, double-bladed tool that resembles a medium-sized melon baller that has been stretched to a sharp point. Made from galvanized steel, its edges are razor sharp and can be resharpened. A peach pitter makes removing blemishes and coring quince almost effortless (I said "almost"!). Although it is rarely recognized, even by professional chefs, I soon discovered that virtually every Armenian cook in the San Joaquin Valley has one stashed in her kitchen utility drawer. Hence, I've taken to calling it the "Fresno Armenian Ladies' Kitchen Widget." I won't cook quince without it. Peach pitters are available on my website (see SOURCES).

---

* Nonreactive equipment and utensils are items made from glass, stainless steel, enamel-coated steel, iron, or wood.

Cultivation and Varieties

I planted a quince tree in Rhode Island, not far from Anne Hutchinson's colony of quince-loving settlers. A delicately branched bare-root seedling arrived from Pennsylvania, and a gardening buddy helped me dig a hole in a sunny, sea-breeze-protected location generous enough to accommodate a full-sized tree.

Within days of planting, a network of neighbors, friends, and fruit growers from Rhode Island, Vermont, Philadelphia, and California began taking an active interest in the little tree's health and survival. Neighbors offered to water it in my absence, and they began to take pictures and send me progress reports. "The quince tree has leaves!" said one neighbor. An overly optimistic update even claimed the young tree had a tiny blossom. Once established, quince trees do have pretty white or pink spring flowers. A friend sent me a tree guard, complete with setup instructions. Another donated nylon stockings, so the tree could be secured to support stakes without the fear of girdling. Soon names poured in—Quincy, Dr. Quince, and my favorite, QT.

With as little as 150 square feet (10 × 15 feet) of green space, even city dwellers can enjoy a quince tree as one of the landscape elements in the garden. Backyard orchards are making a comeback across America today. Popular food movements such as the local-food movement, the sustainable movement, the organic movement, and the slow-food movement all stress the benefits of eating food grown locally. A local orchard guarantees freshness and also provides an economical solution to rising food costs. Even with the pitfalls, there's nothing better than cooking and eating fruit grown in your own backyard.

The fruit-bearing quince, *Cydonia oblonga,* is a member of the rose family, like the apple and pear. Because the fruiting orchard quince is so little known today, especially in the United States, it is often mistaken for the more popular Japanese flowering quince (*Chaenomeles species*), prized for its early spring pink-coral blossoms. Mature flowering quinces will fruit, but the fruit is not generally usable in the kitchen.

The fruit-bearing quince possesses qualities that make it an excellent ornamental and productive choice.

The tree is naturally dwarf, growing 12 to 15 feet tall. The branches tend to be gnarled and angular, which etch beautiful patterns against winter-bare landscapes. They leaf out in early spring with sturdy deep-green, almost sharp-edged leaves. The underbellies of its leaves are silver-colored and have a soft, fuzzy coat like the fruit. The tree flickers green-silver even in the slightest breeze.

Depending on variety, pink or white flowers generally open the spring after planting. Quinces bloom a week or so later than apple trees, making them a good choice for farmers who want to entice pollinating bees to stay longer on their land. Soon after pollination, flower buds swell to small, hard, fuzzy, green-yellow globes that continue to get larger during the growing season. Harvests range from Labor Day well into November depending on the quince variety, but in all cases, as the leaves transition to autumn gold, the fruit ripens more yellow than green and becomes increasingly fragrant, with a distinctive rose-like aroma.

Quince trees are independent, hardy, abundant producers. All varieties are self-pollinating. They grow where most apples do. In 1900, the Brown family planted the largest quince orchard in the world on their farm located in upper New York State along the south shore of Lake Ontario, currently known as apple country. Brown's Berry Patch still grows quince today.

Quince trees require only 200 to 300 "chill hours" (the number of hours during which the temperature falls between 32°F and 45°F) in order to produce fruit. Bare-root cultivars often produce fruit in the second growing season, and definitely by the third. Good yields measure about 33 pounds per mature tree. The trees like full sun and grow best out of the wind. They prefer a lean nitrogen diet, do well in moderately heavy soil, and hate wet feet.

Another alluring feature of the quince for backyard orchardists is that once picked, fresh quinces continue to ripen off the vine and resist spoilage. You can place them in your favorite fruit bowl and enjoy the fragrant centerpiece for weeks. The effects of aging seem to be that the fruit continues to turn an even richer yellow-gold color, and the flesh softens a bit. Of the thousands of quinces in my care over the years, I've had very few go bad, even four months after harvest. That's sturdy fruit!

The downside of caring for orchard quinces is that they require light, regular pruning and are susceptible to many of the same fungi and pests that affect apples and other fruit trees: fire blight, orange rust, bitter pit, borers, and the especially problematic codling moth worm. However, once a tree becomes established, many insect infestations such as aphid attacks subside, and bagging the baby fruit immediately after spring thinning provides adequate protection from the codling moth and its larvae.

Growing good fruit at home helps us appreciate the long history and culture of the varieties we favor. It makes waiting for beloved fruits to ripen all the sweeter. No other fruit tree symbolizes the continuity of civilization quite like the quince. Celebrate the continuity of life; plant a quince tree!

Five Ways to Propagate Fruiting Quince

- Purchase a bare-root quince tree from a reputable nursery (see SOURCES) and plant according to the directions. This method ensures getting the variety desired. A nursery tree will bear fruit the second or third season.

- Graft a scion (dormant twig containing buds from the previous season's growth) onto commercial quince rootstock or an existing quince tree of a different variety. Organizations that promote growing your own fruit (see SOURCES) often hold scion swaps. Proud quince owners are generally happy to provide scions from their trees.

- Transfer a sucker. Quince rootstocks tend to produce suckers, which are shoots that sprout from the shallow roots of a tree. Once sprouted, suckers so desire to become trees that they quickly send out roots of their own. Suckering is a characteristic of fruit-bearing quince that requires regular tending to keep the tree healthy—but advantageous for people desiring their own tree. Dig up the sucker as close to the parent tree as possible when dormant, and plant it in a new location.

- Quince easily roots from healthy, dormant 6 inch cuttings from the previous season's wood. Dip the cut end of the cutting into rooting hormone and plant it in a pot set on a heat mat to stimulate rooting. In a few weeks, plant the rooted cutting outdoors once the danger of frost has passed.

- Quince can be grown from seeds, although not all seedlings will produce quality fruit and it may take more than 5 years for the tree to bear fruit. Place clean quince seeds in damp peat moss and refrigerate for 3 months in a plastic bag, then transfer to indoor pots. When the seedlings are 6 inches tall, plant in the ground after the danger of frost has passed. Growing seedlings is largely done to select new varieties.

Note: Quince has been used as a dwarfing rootstock for pears for over six centuries. If a pear grafted to a quince rootstock has been damaged or killed and the quince rootstock grows into a new plant, the fruit produced on the new quince tree may or may not be of good quality.

Quince Varieties

Today in the United States, quince is best known in California. The fruit has long fascinated California growers, especially those located in the San Joaquin Valley. Most of the country's commercial production is done by a handful of growers in Fresno and Tulare counties, many of whom claim Armenian origin. Other than the United States, Turkey, Armenia, Iran, Greece, Chile, and Australia lead production worldwide.

The USDA Agriculture Research Service lists more than two dozen known varieties of fruit-bearing quince. Listed here are those available commercially.

Pineapple: Developed and introduced by Luther Burbank in Santa Rosa, California, in 1899, the pineapple quince is the most commonly grown commercial variety in the United States today. It is large, more globular than pear-shaped, and slightly aromatic. The raw pulp has a distinctive pineapple-like flavor. The flowers are white, with just a hint of pink. The pineapple quince ripens earlier than other varieties, beginning in late August.

Smyrna: Horticulturist and parks commissioner R. C. Roeding of Fresno, California, brought the Smyrna quince to the United States from Smyrna, now Ismir, Turkey, in 1887. It boasts pretty pink blossoms and large, round-oblong fruit that often possesses irregular ridges on the surface. It ripens from mid-October to mid-November in California. The ripe fruit is pleasingly fragrant, bright yellow-golden in color, and an excellent keeper, storing longer than other quince cultivars when refrigerated.

Orange: Orange quinces are a group rather than a distinct genotype. Their origin is uncertain. Orange quince fruit is apple-shaped and was often called *apple quince*. The blossoms are white and the fruit ranges from large to very large, weighing up to 1 pound. Harvest months in the northeastern United States begin at the end of September, but may be as late as November in California. The tree is vigorous, hardy, and productive.

Champion: Champion quince trees are not sold very often in the United States, but are worthy of mention because they are grown in Chile and the fruit is imported to the United States from April through June. They are medium-sized, are round-oblong shaped, and have excellent flavor.

TEAM QUINCE

On my journey to explore the wonders of growing and cooking with quince, I've met many folks, both young and old, commercial growers and backyard orchard enthusiasts, professional chefs and home cooks, who, without prompting, exclaim, "I love quince!" All seem to agree that it's time to restore the neglected quince to its rightful place in our gardens and on our tables, both in the United States and around the world.

Team Quince is designed to do just that. Armed with the recipes and information contained in *Simply Quince*, we now have a starting point. Team Quince is a virtual community of quince lovers who would love you to join us. Go to my website, **www.queenofquince.com**, read my blog, and join the party—exchange recipes, share personal experiences, report quince news, search for unidentified varieties in your area, and connect with people in your own neighborhood and around the globe, who share your interest and passion for the quince. Do it today. I'd love to meet and work with you!

Sources

Fruit Products and Kitchen Ware:

Amazon.com
Gourmet Food Department
www.amazon.com

Kalustyan's
123 Lexington Avenue
New York, NY 10016
(212) 685-3888
www.kalustyans.com

Queen of Quince Products
P.O. Box 51637
Pacific Grove, CA 93950
(831) 655-4377
www.queenofquince.com

Nurseries

Boyer Nurseries & Orchards, Inc.
405 Boyer Nursery Road
Biglerville, PA 17307
(717) 677-8558
www.boyernurseries.com

Hidden Springs Nursery
170 Hidden Springs Lane
Cookeville, TN 38501
(931) 268-2592
www.hiddenspringsnursery.com

J. E. Miller Nurseries
5060 West Lake Road
Canadaigua, NY 14424
(800) 836-9630
www.millernurseries.com

One Green World
28696 S. Cramer Road
Molalla, OR 97038
(877) 353-4028; (503) 651-3005
www.onegreenworld.com

Raintree Nursery
391 Butts Road
Morton, WA 98356
(360) 496-6400
www.raintreenursery.com

Trees of Antiquity
20 Wellsona Road
Paso Robles, CA 93446
(805) 467-9909
www.treesofantiquity.com

ORGANIZATIONS

California Rare Fruit Growers
66 Farragut Avenue
San Francisco, CA   94112
www.crfg.org

Home Orchard Society
P.O. Box 230192
Tigard, OR 97281
www.homeorchardsociety.org

North American Fruit Explorers (NAFEX)
1716 Apples Road
Chapin, IL   62628
(217)245-7589
www.nafex.org

USDA Agriculture Research Service
National Clonal Germplasm Repository
33447 Peoria Road
Corvallis, OR 97333
(541) 738-4200
www.ars.usda.gov/pwa/corvallis/ncgr

Weights and Measures

Fresh Quince Size Chart

	Weight	Comparative Size	Pulp Equivalent (cups)
Large	9 oz. to >1 lb. avg. 10 to 12 oz.	Softball	2 to 2 ½ cups
Medium	6 to 9 oz. avg. 8 oz.	Baseball	1 to 1½ cups
Small	3½ to 6 oz. avg. 4½ oz.	Tennis ball	1 cup or less

Temperature Equivalents

Fahrenhite to Celsius (Centigrade)

32	0	freezing
68	20	room temp.
212	100	boiling
300	149	
325	162	
350	177	
375	190	
400	205	
425	218	
450	232	
500	260	

Liquid Equivalents

Cups and spoonfuls	Metric
1 teaspoon (tsp.)	5 ml
1 tablespoon (tbs.)	15 ml
⅛ cup (1 oz.)	30 ml
¼ cup (2 oz.)	62 ml
⅓ cup	80 ml
½ cup (4 oz.)	125 ml
⅔ cup	160 ml
¾ cup (6 oz.)	180 ml
1 cup (8 oz.)	250 ml
2 cups (1 pint / 16 oz.)	500 ml or ½ liter
4 cups (1 quart / 32 oz.)	1,000 ml or 1 liter

Weight Equivalents

Pounds (lbs.) & Ounces (oz.)	Metric
1 ounce	28.3 grams
¼ pounds (4 ounces)	113.5 grams
½ pound (8 ounces)	227 grams
1 pound (16 ounces)	454 grams
2.2 pounds	1 kilogram

To convert ounces to grams, multiply ounces by 28.3495.
To convert grams to ounces, multiply grams by 0.035274.

Index

and quince with walnuts conserve, 122

Cream cheese

and ricotta cheese tart, with poached quince, 152

Crème anglaise, baked quince, orange-glazed, topping for, 178

Crisps/crumbles

cranberry-quince vanilla crunch, 138

sour cherry-quince-almond crisp, 140

Currants

in fresh ginger and quince pomegranate chutney, 107

in quince and parnip stew, 87

Custard

quince clafouti, 157

D

Duck breasts, pan-braised, with quince-sambal chutney, 95

F

Feta cheese, and heirloom tomatoes, poached quince

salad, 57

Fruit leather

poaching liquid for, 28

quince, 117

G

Ginger, fresh

and quince in pomegranate vinegar chutney, 107

and quince marmalade, 120

in mashed yams and quince, 71

in quick quince chutney, 109

in quince-apple-peach compote, 135

in quince relish, 110

in quince-sambal chutney, for duck breasts, 95

in turkey chili with quince, 85

Goat cheese, and poached quince, watercress, red onion, salad, 51

Gouda cheese (Danish), and casaba melon, prosciutto salad with quince vinegar, 50

Grand Marnier, ice cream with quince paste, 181

Grappa, quince-infused, 183

Gruyere cheese, and quince paste sandwich, grilled, 175

H

Halibut, and poached quince in phyllo, 97

Haloumi cheese, and quince paste sandwich, grilled, 175

History

biblical references, 14

cultivation, 14

Greek sources, 14–15

in the New World, 16–17

medieval European sources, 15–16

migration of, 14–17

Roman sources, 15

Honey

in cumin-glazed carrots and quince, 68

in mashed yams and quince with fresh ginger, 71

in medicinal tea, 35

in orange glaze, for baked quinces, 178

I

Ice cream, Grand Marnier with quince paste, 181

J

Jalapeño pepper

in cilantro, yogurt sauce, for curried lamb and quince stuffed wontons, 44

in halibut and poached quince-stuffed phyllo, 97

Q

R

S

Vinegar, quince
    casaba melon and prosciutto salad, for, 50
    with grilled chicken and poached quince, for Cobb
        salad, 53
Vodka
    quince-infused, 184
    quince-infused, toddy, 185

W
Walnuts
    and mascarpone cheese, quince preserves in katayif
        pastry, 165
    Grand Marnier ice cream, topping for, 181
    in cinnamon-spiced quince paste, 34
    in quince and cranberry conserves, 122
    in stuffing, for baked quince, 29
    -quince pâté, open-faced sandwiches with arugula, 42

with quince fruit leather, 117
Watercress
    and poached quince, red onion salad, 51
    and shrimp, poached quince salad, 55
White kidney bean, and poached quince, pancetta salad, 58
Wontons, curried quince and lamb stuffed, 44

Y
Yams
    mashed with quince and ginger, 71
    with pork tenderloin, quince, butternut squash, 91
Yogurt
    and cilantro dipping sauce, for lamb and quince stuffed
        wontons, 44
    lamb-stuffed quince, topping for, 93
Yogurt cheese, quince and Asian pear compote, topping
    for, 133

Photograph by Lisa Fucile

About Barbara Ghazarian
"The Queen of Quince"

A true original, Barbara Ghazarian capitalizes on her award-winning cookbook, *Simply Armenian: Naturally Healthy Ethnic Cooking Made Easy* (Mayreni, 2004), with the first tribute to the quince in culinary history.

Like her Armenian grandmother before her, she is passionate about growing and cooking quince—a fruit cultivated since the time of Noah and whose origin traces back to the Caucasus Mountains region of Armenia.

A native of New England, Barbara Ghazarian currently splits her time between Monterey, California, and Newport, Rhode Island, where she planted a quince tree, named QT, which is cared for by TEAM QUINCE friends and neighbors.

NOTES

NOTES

NOTES